SERIOUS FUN

STORIES, POEMS and PICTURES from

BARRETSTOWN

SERIOUS

FUN

STORIES, POEMS and PICTURES from

BARRETSTOWN

EDITOR **TIM O'DEA**

FOREWORD **PAUL NEWMAN**

DIARY EXTRACTS **Dr PAUL ZELTZER**

GILL & MACMILLAN

Gill & Macmillan Ltd
Hume Avenue, Park West, Dublin 12
with associated companies throughout the world
www.gillmacmillan.ie
© Barretstown Gang Camp Fund Ltd, 2005
© Diary extracts by Paul Zeltzer, 2005
0 7171 3912 3
Compiled by Emer Ryan
Design and print origination by Graham Thew Design
Colour reproduction by Typeform Ltd, Dublin
Printed by GraphyCems Ltd, Spain

This book is typeset in Bell Gothic, Monotype Modern and Yellabelly

The paper used in this book comes from the wood pulp of managed forests.
For every tree felled, at least one tree is planted, thereby renewing natural
resources.

A CIP catalogue record for this book is available from the British Library.

5 4 3 2 1

CONTENTS

Foreword by Paul Newman   vi

F-U-N Spells Barretstown!   5

Friends for Life   33

Magical Tales from Barretstown Castle   47

Olympic Dreams   79

The Nature Room   89

Here's a Funny Story...   115

'Freddy — The Frog who Couldn't
Quack' and Other Animal Tales   131

The Secret Garden   159

'Roger the Pirate' and Other
Adventure Stories   173

In a World of My Own   203

Foreword

BY **PAUL NEWMAN**

I am frequently asked what motivated me to start the first Hole in the Wall Camp in 1988, and, while I would like to have something noble and inspiring to say about the origins of the Camps, the simple truth of the matter is that I wanted to acknowledge the role luck plays in everyone's life — the beneficence of it in the lives of many, such as myself, and the random brutality of it in the lives of others, particularly children, who might not have a lifetime to make up for it.

What else can one call it when a child is diagnosed with cancer, HIV/AIDS, or some other life-threatening condition? It is just devastatingly bad luck. Such conditions create physical pain and limitations, but, also, can terrorise a child and isolate him or her from the very experience of childhood. This need not be.

At The Hole in the Wall Camps, we have a saying that there is *no such thing as a sick child*, but *just a child who happens to be sick*. Take that thinking and mix it with 75 to 100 children per session in a Camp environment, and the result is plenty of noise, energy, confidence building, and, wham! — the child re-emerges.

Barretstown is a great example of what I mean by good luck. How fortuitous was the extraordinary generosity of the Irish government to offer this very special place for our first venture beyond the shores of America. I will not forget my initial visit to the property at Ballymore Eustace. Walking through the castle and the stable courtyard, I could begin to see and hear the place swarming with scores of children having a grand time in the magical ambience of a medieval carnival. I knew right there and then that Barretstown was perfect.

Now, thanks to the hard work and generosity of so many from throughout Ireland, Europe and the US, the reality is every bit as exciting as the dream. Since Barretstown first opened its doors in 1994, and through 2004, over 10,000 children have come to Barretstown from over 25 different countries for the time of their lives. Thousands of volunteer Caras have looked out for them, doctors and nurses have given freely of their time to assure a medically safe and supportive environment, and untold numbers of donors have kept the doors open free of charge to the families.

What great good fortune that our first international venture was Barretstown. It has given us the confidence and experience to continue to develop new Camps in Europe, Africa and the Middle East, with more on the way.

If the first Camp in Connecticut, USA, is the founder of The Hole in the Wall movement, then Barretstown deserves to be thought of as the founder of The Hole in the Wall International movement.

I thank all of you who have made Barretstown possible, and all of you who will continue to make Barretstown a possibility for thousands of children.

Acknowledgements

Thanks are due to **Fergal Tobin** and **all at Gill & Macmillan** for making this project a reality and enabling Barretstown to share some of the magic with the 'outside world'.

Thanks to **Paul Zeltzer** for his commitment to Barretstown and for allowing us to include his diary from camp in this book. A massive thank you to **Hilary Makin** for using her talents to edit the text of the diary.

Thanks to **Alex Singer** for sifting through the stories from years gone by and adapting to typing in different languages.

A special note of thanks must go to **GlaxoSmithKline** for their continued support.

Finally, none of this would happen without **the children** who come to Barretstown and **the staff** who work with them and make the impossible possible. They are the magic that is Barretstown.

Barretstown would like to thank all our supporters over the past 11 years for enabling us to continue the work we are doing for children with cancer and other serious illnesses.

A Barretstown Doctor's Diary

THE DAY BEFORE DAY ONE!

The summer has peaked and mid-August beckons me to Ireland. As I have done for the last nine summers, I am about to leave Los Angeles and in eight hours land at Dublin Airport. I wonder what this next ten days will present. In one way it has become 'ordinary'. After all, my ninth summer as a Camp Doctor for children with cancer and blood diseases will probably not offer any medical challenges I have not seen before.

I know that 95 per cent of the visits that will come to the 'Medshed' (the Camp's medical clinic facility) will be for insect bites, rashes, stomach aches due to unfamiliar surroundings and food and… So why do I do it? Why has it become a ritual?

The runway speeds by more slowly and then I disembark, make my way through the terminal, and go through passport inspection. The friendly Irish accent of the officer triggers faint memories of cardinal camp events that then start to flood back.

I think of Orla, a proud, stately and beautiful 15-year-old from inner-city Dublin. Never having been allowed to be a child, she had to be both mum to her 6-year-old sister and mother to her own HIV-infected mother who was dying. But Orla also had relapsed Acute Myelocytic Leukaemia herself and needed constant platelet and blood transfusions. The disease was ravaging her body and this camp was the only time she could just be 15 years old. During that session in 1996, Dr Jon Finlay and I had a choice — stay or transfer her to the children's hospital in Dublin. We knew that to send her to the hospital would mean she would never experience camp again in her lifetime. We decided to make the Medshed a temporary Intensive Care Unit and give her intravenous fluids and antibiotics. The three nurses volunteered to care for her in shifts overnight.

During the next three days, two events happened with Orla that reminded me why I do return to Camp every year. One of the Caras (meaning 'Friend' in Irish – the name Barretstown gives to volunteers), Patrick, a 40-ish former boxer and also plumber for the castle, brought her breakfast in bed in the Medshed resting rooms where she stayed all night. Dressed up in tuxedo and tails and with his helper manservant (a fellow young camper, Mike) similarly dressed and following him with the toast, he brought in the meal on a silver tray adorned with a yellow rose. The next night, I saw Orla get out from bed in the Medshed, ask for her intravenous lines to be detached, and request that the nurses walk her to the 'Big Dance' in the theatre. With her regal wide-brimmed hat that covered her bare scalp, she danced with her Caras and also her fellow partners in cancer for over an hour. She died two months later.

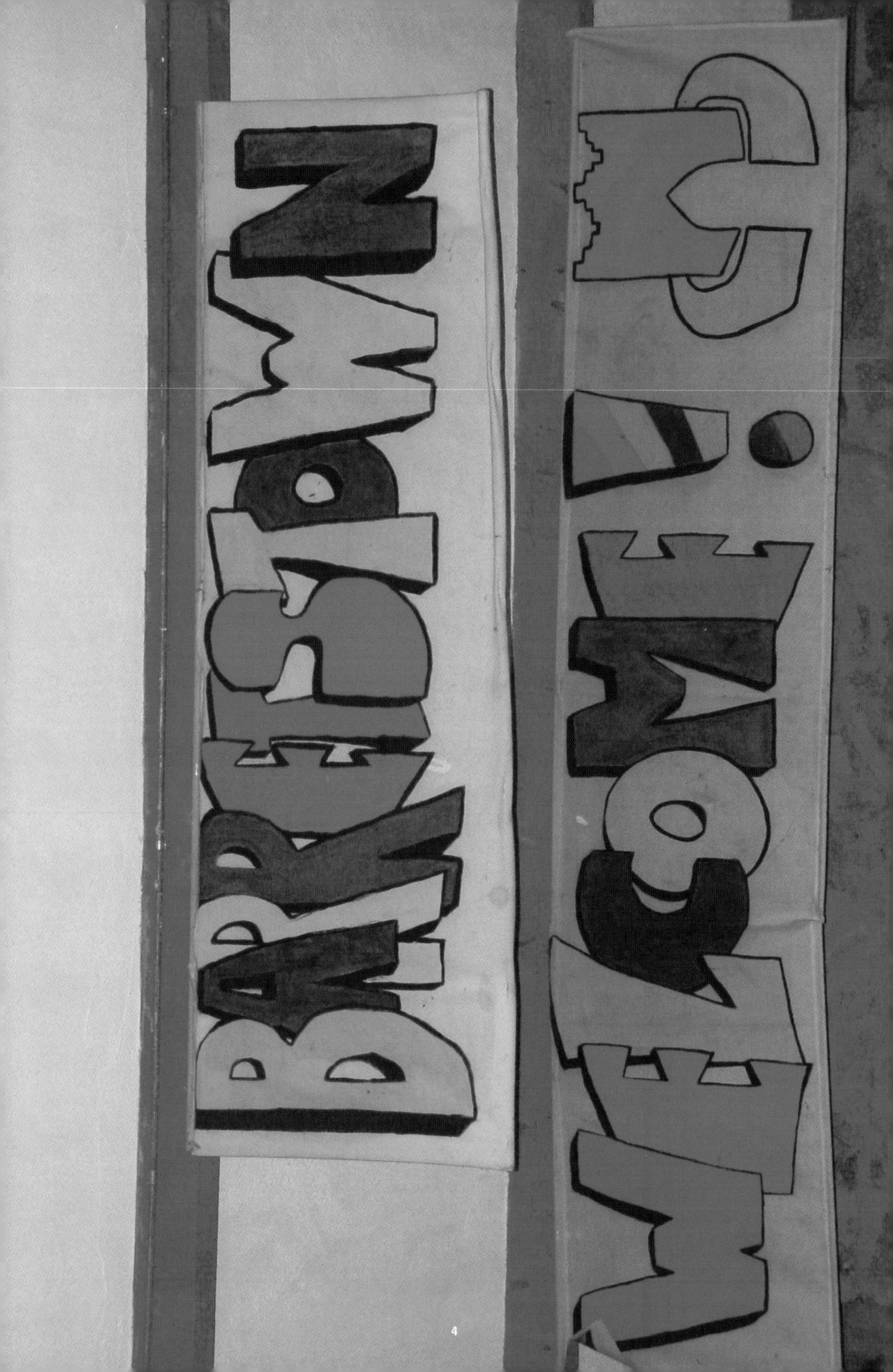

F-U-N
Spells
Barretstown!

In Barretstown it's fun to play,
So many activities every day.
Everybody comes from a different place,
And they all have a smile on their face.
They all agree it's a fun place to stay.

It's always been sunny
And everything's funny
It's all dancey
And everything's fancy
And you don't need money.

Barretstown O Barretstown
There's so much to do
How should I start to tell you?

In crazy and lazies
You can pick daisies
Or try the activities on hand.

There's Adventure (it's really cool).
You can climb the high ropes or just play pool.
PS This camp isn't like school.

The canoes move through the lake,
Watch them pass with a chocolate milkshake.
See the wall that's very tall,
See the fish that's very small.
Find a shell that you can break.

Since the circus came to town,
No one wears a frown.
Everyone dances, everyone sings,
It's such a beautiful thing.
So, put on your shoes and boogie on down.

At Barretstown there's loads of fun,
Excitement and laughter for everyone,
There's lots of games and activities to do,
Which ones to choose, it's up to you.

It's wacky and wild at dinner time,
The Caras hop for our food before we dine,
Then it's time to punish the cheaters,
Clapping and booing the ones that beat us.

There's archery, high ropes, canoeing and fishing,
Trust me, there's nothing you should be missing,
You split into groups and make new friends,
There's tons of laughter, and the fun never ends.

I don't want to leave, cuz I'm having such a great time,
I'll take home memories like never before in my life,
I'll be so disappointed when I've got to pack,
I hope next year I have the chance to come back.

There was a castle
It was big, it had big rooms
There were lots of leaves

Barretstown is good
There are lots of cottages
It is very good.

The New Life of a Camper

The young Kate was a camper and because she spent most of her life in one hospital or another, she used to be very sad. One day when she was a little kid, someone told her that when the summer would finish at the beginning of September, she would go to a camp in Ireland called 'Barretstown'. At this camp kids have a really good time. They do horse riding, archery, fishing, canoeing, theatre, video, photo, football, tennis, basketball, arts and crafts and many other things.

September arrived and Kate went to Barretstown where she had a very good time, but the strange thing was that what she liked the most was the parties they used to have in the cottage at night. She even found a boyfriend there. John was her first and last boyfriend. Two years ago they got married and both of them started to work as Caras at Barretstown.

(Originally in Spanish)

The zipline is cool,
It makes you look like a fool.
I like sitting in the trees,
There's a lovely breeze.
And thank god I don't have to go
  to school.

I like Barretstown,
It makes me laugh like a clown.
I like the people, they are kind
  and share,
They never make you beware.
It never makes me frown.

Brilliante
Amigos
Rockeros
Romantico
Especial
Tormenta
Significativo
Tigresas
Orgulloso
Wou monstuosa
Nuevo

Brilliant
Amazing
Radical
Revitalising
Entertaining
Thrilling
Special
Thoughtful
Overwhelming
Wonderful
Never-ending fun!!

Barretstown is great
It has anything you want
Scotland arrived late

Nature's way of being great
The plants get killed in the end
All the pretty plants.

Fishing

When I cast my long thread line,
I say that fish, that fish is definitely mine.
I waited there with no patience at all,
Watching the fish swim around the bread ball.
I got a small tug and I reeled him in,
When I saw the fish I said hey that fish is thin.
I had it for dinner that night,
And when I was finished it was out of sight.

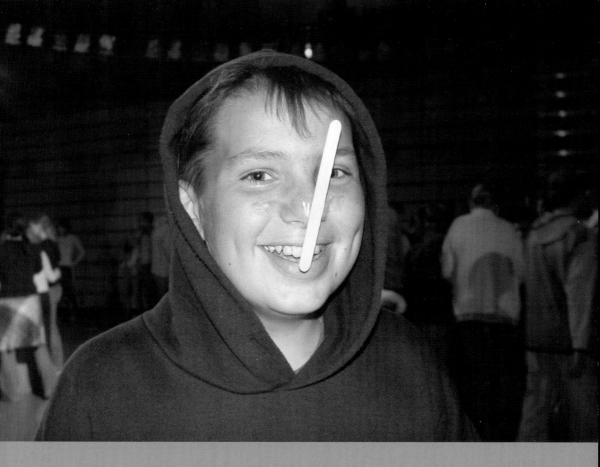

It was a beautiful sight,
When the campfire lit the night.
We had a big dinner,
And a breakfast to get thinner.
The moon was bright,
All through the night.
We slept in tents at night,
And got up in daylight.
We saw fish,
And wanted to put it on our dish.
Rob came and sang a song,
The song was very long.

Beautiful
Activities
Recreation
Rock on
Encourage others
Terrific food
Silly Olympics
Time well spent
Optimistic people
Wildly wonderful
Night-time chats

When you go to Barretstown
You never go home with a frown
With all the fun stories and friends
The fun, joy and craziness never ends
In this place you never feel down.

I love the laughter and games
But it's hard to learn all the names
With all the hopping at meals
You love how it feels
To see all your cool photos in frames.

Day One

11 a.m.

After loading my suitcase and those of fourteen Italian boys and girls on the gaily-decorated Barretstown bus, we have a one-hour ride from the airport to the seventeenth-century castle called Barretstown. This is an idyllic 500-acre estate on the rolling hills and dales of Kildare, 40 miles south of Dublin.

The 14 Italian campers who accompanied me in the bus had arrived from Milan at the same time I did. Aged 7 to 12 years old, they are chaperoned by Luca, a Paediatric Oncologist from Genoa, and Marta, the secretary of the Rangoni Foundation which organised the funds to send these children to camp. Using my best restaurant Italian and Luca his best English, we realise that we know many oncologists in common though this is our first meeting. With Marta leading, the boys and girls dressed in Rangoni T-shirts and red baseball caps are singing songs and playing games the entire hour.

12.45 p.m.

Passing the gates and entering the $^1/_4$-mile sweeping drive up to the castle, the children begin to be transformed — sheep, horses and finally the turrets of the castle appear. There on the driveway in front of the castle are 50 staff in hats, shorts and T-shirts, wildly hooting, cheering, waving and trumpeting, welcoming these young heroes from illness.

After a warm Irish hug and a kiss from Barretstown Clinical Coordinator Eimear, introductions to the four volunteer nurses follow: Paulina from Vancouver, Cara from Seattle, Joni from Denver and Helen from Dublin. My partner oncologist, Maria from Pamplona, greets me and I get another warm hug, a kiss on each cheek, and I say: 'Que marvelosa!' I speak some Spanish, so this should be fun. Eimear says that this camp session is a big one, larger than I have ever experienced: 102 children to check in!

Leaving the castle courtyard and the Caras who are unloading the suitcases and backpacks, it's off to the Medshed to begin the real work of the day.

I imagine the anxiety of each of those mothers and fathers, who make the choice to pack their child off to a foreign land, taking the risk that some nurse or physician who does not know their child, their painful history of life and death struggles with each chemotherapy course or emergency surgery, will truly care for their child as they would do.

1 p.m.

The Italian children do not seem to be phased by the newness of the Caras, their grown-up and larger-than-life camp leaders, or the new routine of sitting at the thirteen large tables in the huge open-beamed dining hall. The camp director, Jules, announces that the Caras will have a one-legged hopping contest to the kitchen, and each one will bring back each cottage's plates of food to their table. The children squeal in delight watching their Cara leaping out, wanting to be the first one back with their meal. More on camp rules later…

3 p.m.

Checking in

This begins the real work of the day and probably is the most intensive and time-consuming activity for all the Medshed staff. It consists of talking with each camper and their translator, if necessary, to document if they are on any chemotherapy, antibiotics, blood-support medications, anti-histamines, and so on. We ask the children about their medical history, interesting adventures on the plane trip, where they are from, how many siblings, etc.

Every cream, pill, bottle or container the children have brought with them must be examined, recorded, and prescriptions written for their dose, timing, and how administered. This information is coded onto a medication record specific for each child. Eventually, the 50 per cent or so children who come to camp on active chemotherapy will receive their pills on time in the dining room or in their cottage. Some prefer to come to the Medshed.

We have checked in all the fourteen Italian children plus the ten Irish kids who were driven by their parents by car.

5 p.m.

Next, before dinner at 6 p.m., will be the ten children from Manchester and southern coastal cities who flew in from London an hour ago. Only three suitcases are missing. Thank goodness their nurses know to carry their medications in hand-luggage!

9 p.m.

The twelve children from Cyprus arrive and their translator, Maria, leads them into the Medshed, carrying the huge canvas athletic bag full of their medications. The children are quiet after the long flight; none has been here before. Maria, the chaperone and translator, has been to Barretstown on three previous occasions and knows the routine well. She accompanies the children, one at a time, into the examining rooms for me and Maria (Doctora) to interview and examine. She also translates the labels on the medicine bottles and some of the physicians' notes.

10.40 p.m.

The fourteen children, chaperones and translators from the Madrid flight arrive. Maria (my Spanish physician partner) knows some of the boys as they are from Pamplona where she practises. I get to try out my Spanish!

Totals

102 children have been checked in and our nurse and physician team has personally interviewed and examined 55 who are on active treatment. So far, no major infections, problems related to the journey from home, minor infections or untreated pain are in evidence.

Friends
for
Life

You have guardian angels in life,
Good parents and good friends.
Love the first,
Adore the second.
But never forget the third.

(Originally in Hungarian)

Sam,
Fun to be with, up for anything, caring and happy
Daughter of the best mother,
Who loves cats, hot weather and shopping,
Who is scared of heights, spiders and insects,
Who wants to see New Zealand, the end of wars and my uncle's
lamb.

My Experience

When I first went to camp I did not know anyone, I was really scared. Everyone was in the theatre and I found it was really hard to approach anyone, as I didn't know what language they spoke.

Finally, I met an Irish boy who was in my cottage. I felt a little better then. At first I couldn't wait to go home, but after a few days I was really enjoying the camp. I was enjoying it so much that I went on the stage at the disco and performed as the Spice Girls. Then next night was the Cabaret and I did one show with my group and another with four people in my cottage.

I have really enjoyed my time at camp and now that I have to go home in one day, I really do not want to leave.

Do you remember when we were playing together?
How good it was!
Let us try to be friends again!
It would be great!
We should not argue so much!
It would be great, wouldn't it?
Let us try it again!

When the world looks at you,

And love chooses you,

I will come tomorrow,

And the flower will bloom,

I love you,

I like and admire you,

But a few days ago,

We were separated by treasures,

It was dark,

Our friendship came to an end,

Today I'm asking you for

Love and friendship,

So that treasure never tears us apart again,

And so that treasure never casts a shadow upon us.

(Originally in Polish)

39

Alone

Morning,
Mid-day,
And evening
People are alone.

No family,
No friends,
Not even a roof
Over their heads.

Morning,
Mid-day,
And evening
Animals are alone.

People find their love,
Animals find their love.
Now nobody is alone
Any more.

When you come first,
You are sad and lonely.
But people like Caras and people like friends
Help us all to meet each other and
When we are sad or when we are lonely,
The Caras tell us not to be sad.
They tuck us in at night and meet us early and bright.
I was sad to leave my home
But I had a great time at Barretstown.

This time last year
Was so bad.
My younger brother was diagnosed,
With an illness no one knew he had.

Those first few weeks were hard to take,
Kept wishing it was all a horrible mistake.
Why him?
Over and over I thought,
This innocent boy.
Did not cause this distraught.
Being brought to the hospital,
Injected, X-rayed.
Every day I'd see his discarded football,
In the yard where he no longer played.

Everybody was so nice and still
There was a gap inside me,
That I could not fill.
Then I came to this camp,
And finally could
Talk to people my own age,
Who really understood.

I could never really say that there
Was an advantage to someone having cancer.
But if there was,
Barretstown would be the answer.

During the daytime
You are prettier than the sun
By night prettier than the moon
And my wish is to give you
A tender kiss

Children ask for toys
Prisoners ask for freedom
And I ask for plenty of happiness for her

Donald is a duck
Mickey is a mouse
And Kitty-cat's eyes
Are my heart.

(Originally in Spanish)

Day Two

9 a.m.

Breakfast and, in fact, all meals at Barretsown are different from
most camps. First, we have Declan, our chef. Healthy bran, muesli,
granola or oatmeal, whole grain breads, decadent Coco Pops, eggs,
bacon, sausages, croissants better than any French bakery … yumm.
Sensitivity to vegetarian and special diets also must be available for
each meal.

Announcement time. Jules the camp director briefly tells the children
about the seven do's and don'ts at camp. Each one is acted out in
pantomime by one of the Caras. Then, unique to Barretstown, each of the
translators, up at the podium with Jules, gives their children the
translation in their native language. This session, we hear Jules'
spiel translated into Spanish, Greek, Arabic and Italian. A cynic would
say this could never work … but it does, and effortlessly.

10.15 a.m.

I note that Luca, the Italian physician with whom I sat on the bus
coming in and who is acting as a translator and Cara, is leading two
of his pre-teen boys down the hall into an examining room. He is using
this as an opportunity to teach one of the haemophiliac boys to self-
infuse. Apparently at home his mother or a nurse has always given his
anti-clotting factor infusion in his vein. In the true spirit of the
Barretstown adventure, this boy wants to try, for the first time, to
start his own IV and give himself the injection. This 10-year-old
organises all his equipment: needle and tubing, alcohol pads, rubber
constriction band to pump up his veins — all the things he has seen
others do for him since he was 2 years old. There in an examining room
built for three people where myself, Luca, a watchful and astonished
Irish Cara, and three cottage buddies giving directions on how to aim
the needle, all crowd around the seated boy with his arm outstretched
with veins bulging — anticipating the first stick. In English and
Italian, 'Lift the needle.' 'Aim it more to the left.' 'Go slowly.'
'No, lift and move it more to the right.' Suddenly there is the reward
of red fluid inching up the thin tube from the needle and there is a
group inhalation and sigh. Next, Luca attaches the syringe with 1,000

units of Factor 8 which is to be one of three injections that week.
The boy proudly holds and then applies pressure to the syringe shaft,
erasing the red colour as the infusion that will prevent life-
threatening bleeding enters his vein painlessly.

In five minutes, he, with a plaster over his site of triumph, and
the entourage walk out of the room and down the hall to the waiting
area. Word must have travelled via a mode I will never understand; he
receives a standing ovation from the fifteen or twenty campers, Caras
and nurses who are milling around the waiting room of the Medshed
awaiting post-breakfast medications and antibiotic creams before going
out for the first morning camp activity.

12.45 p.m.

Children's screams of laughter, mirth, joy and play rise up from below
the windows of my corner bedroom. I look out one side and there are
two Caras and four children taking photos in front of the castle for
the session newsletter that will accompany each child home in nine
days' time. A Jordanian girl, dressed as a 1920s male news reporter
with hat and moustache, is interviewing her Cara. Outside the other
window, I see a group of boys and girls on the soccer pitch (i.e.
castle side lawn): two are dressed as fairy princesses — one complete
with starred wand, one sixteenth-century king complete with mild limp
caused by a brain tumour, a harlequin joker or two, and two English
boys from Manchester in shorts and camp T-shirts and not conscious or
aware of their chemotherapy-caused baldness. All are rehearsing a play
for the talent show in a week's time. Camp has started in full swing
and cancer has retreated, for a while.

(Day Two is continued on p. 76.)

Magical
Tales from
Barretstown
Castle

The White Wizard and the Black Witch

Once upon a time, in a really faraway country where witches and wizards lived and did magic, one day, a witch came and made a spell that took their magic from them forever.

Scared, they went into the country to ask the wise animals for help, but they could not help them. Then they decided to go to the gnomes' tree to make up a plan to take the witch powers away. So they went to the witch's house.

Once they were there, they told the witch they wanted the power she had stolen to be

returned. The oldest wizard of all asked the gnomes for their potion, and put it into a wand, but even then it didn't work.

Then the wizard decided to make the potion himself. He collected many things that he put into it, such as a green frog, a mouse, an elephant's eye, four flies and a scarf from the witch. He put all this into his wand. He went into the witch's house and he took her powers away.

Then he told her to go away forever to some other house, never to come back.

4,000 years ago there lived Ureka Chocalocalus. He was a great ruler of Egypt and Greece but was born in Ireland.

Ureka was really a mean ruler because he kept some of the taxes for himself. And the men were not strong enough to defeat Ureka so the girls had him hung, drawn and quartered and they got a reward and paid the money back to the people.

WHY THE SUN ALWAYS SHINES IN BARRETSTOWN

Once upon a time, there were three gods, called Rose God of beauty, Arthur God of the Sea and Perfect God of Sweets. One made sweets, one made beauty and one made storms all the time.

Rose and Perfect were friends and Arthur was their enemy. Rose and Perfect did not like Arthur because he made storms all the time and they blew away the sweets and wrecked their make-up and Rose's blond hair. So Rose phoned Rainbow, God of the Sky, and asked him to phone Natural to get back at Arthur. Natural made the sea change colour and the rain change colour which made Arthur mad. Arthur then rang Zola to see if he would help him. Arthur said, 'Will you help me by making a fire in the forest to make Rose, Perfect and Natural mad?'

'No,' said Zola, 'because my brother Guilt is the God of the Trees and I just can't disobey him, but if you want, I can make a fire somewhere else. For example, I can make it in the sky.'

Later that night he put a fire in the sky. Sunshine Aclures, God of Daylight, saw the fire and told her friends Rose, Natural, Perfect and Rainbow about the fire and they were all very mad. They were all up that night trying to make a potion to stop the fire from spreading anywhere else. They finally figured out a potion to turn the fire into the sun. They held the fire with a big ring and that's why the sun always shines in Barretstown.

Happy Ever After

Once upon a time, there was a beautiful princess who lived in a huge castle. She was very beautiful and rich. Many men asked for her hand in marriage. All were refused. One of these was King Robert, an evil sneaky man. So one night he kidnapped the princess and locked her in his castle. She still refused to marry him. Prince John heard of the kidnapping and knew who it was. He travelled for days and days until he reached the king's castle. He fought King Robert in a long, hard battle. In the end, good overcame evil and the princess was saved and she married the prince and lived happily ever after.

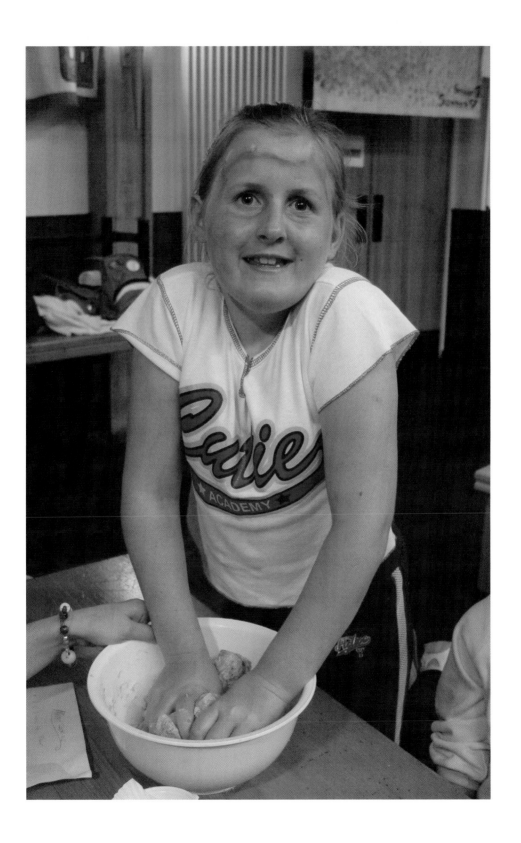

In 1218, there was a witch who killed a princess a day before she was going to get married to a handsome prince. The witch disguised herself as the princess and married the prince. Three days afterwards the witch cast a spell on the king to hate the prince. The king killed the prince and the witch disguised herself as another very pretty lady and came to the king and said that his daughter had drowned herself and would he like to marry her to keep him company. But while all this was happening a guard heard the witch singing, 'Ha I'm going to rule this country soon! I killed the princess and the prince and soon I will kill the king ha ha ha!' And the guard told the king and the king was very mad. And when the witch came back to ask if he had decided, the king said, 'Kill her, kill her now!' So the witch was killed and still haunts the castle saying, 'I will get you sooner or later!'

A long time ago there was a young man called John Buckman the III. He lived in Barretstown Castle 300 years ago with his twenty children and his fiancée named Elizabeth. One late night, John woke up and saw a shadow creeping down the stairs. John drew out his sword and went out on the landing. The intruder came back upstairs and took out his sword to fight John. The fight moved into the main room upstairs. The intruder

jumped to strike John but missed. The sword went through the landing floor. The intruder bent down to pull the sword out of the ceiling but then John turned around and stabbed the intruder.

Today some people say the spirit of the intruder is still walking around Barretstown Castle. It was 1,000 years ago when the Castle was discovered.

The Little Mermaid

Once upon a time there lived seven mermaids. The most beautiful was the youngest.

Their mother told them a story about other mermaids, who lived deep in the ocean. The little mermaid asked her mother if she could go up to the surface. Mum answered, 'Not until you are old enough like your sisters.' Then one of her sisters went up to the surface and the youngest followed her. But unfortunately she was not skilful enough and a shark grabbed her. When she lost consciousness, a little seahorse swam by and saved her life. After that, the seahorse took her to a beach.

A prince was walking there and when he saw the mermaid, he immediately fell in love with her and gave her a kiss.

And they lived happily ever after.

(Originally in Hungarian)

The Enchanted Princess

Once upon a time there was a very good princess. But one day a wicked witch cast a spell on her and turned her into the nastiest princess of all the kingdom. The spell could not be broken unless someone could make her laugh.

So the years went by and the princess became more and more nasty. Until one fine day, a handsome prince with a good sense of humour came to the castle. Days and days passed with no result, but the prince never gave up and in the end he managed to make the princess laugh, breaking the spell. The princess once again became the good person she had always been.

(Originally in Spanish)

Once upon a time there was a king named George who lived in a castle. King George was very mean to all the people who lived in the cottages. He was very handsome and good at sports.

Many years ago there lived a queen, Juana, who was very beautiful. But Queen Monika, who was immortal, put a spell on Queen Juana because she was jealous. The spell turned Juana into a pig. The King was distressed so he married Monika, the witch. At the wedding banquet they had Queen Juana as roast pork. When they finished the meal Monika told the King the truth, that he had eaten his own wife Juana. The King became angry and he ordered Monika to be jailed in the prison. Afterwards the King was very ill and a good fairy appeared before him. She said that she would save Juana if the King treated all the people of Barretstown well. If not, Juana would stay forever a pig.

The King accepted the proposition and he turned into a good king. King George kept on trying to be good but suddenly Monika escaped from the castle prison. Then the witch Monika reappeared and turned George into a hippopotamus. When the people saw him they took him to a zoo in Madrid and he turned from being the king of a country into the king of hippopotamuses. When the good fairy found out what had happened she decided to go to see King George. When she saw him, she understood why the people were so worried about the sudden disappearance of the King. The fairy helped the King to get out of the zoo.

(Originally in Spanish)

An Impossible Story

Once upon a time, there was a little town called Grinfields that was on the Nomembeng Hill.

Princess Hentmire, who was Grinfields' King's daughter, was in love with her servant. He was a handsome boy who the King had bought from a noble in the town not long ago.

Hentmire and her lover, Ronen, had a nice love story hidden from the King and from the rest of the world. They were happy and nobody knew that they loved each other like crazy.

King Coligan was growing older and he realised that there was little time left. His only daughter, Hentmire, wasn't married yet and the King needed to pass his crown to his heir before dying. One day, he organised a hunting trip in the fields of the kingdom. The king waited until all the guests and his daughter were there.

They had just finished dinner and they were all sitting around the table, when the King stood up and said, 'We are here today because there is something that has been making me really anxious for two days now. I have realised that my days as Grinfields' King are nearly finished. For that reason, I have decided that my daughter should marry one of your sons, the one who has noble blood in his veins, in order to make me sure that by the time I am dead, Grinfields Town will be in good hands.'

When he ended his speech, one of the nobles stood up and said, 'I am Edgar, Lord of Francils and Loenbirten County, I would like to offer myself to marry Princess Hentmire, and I swear that I will be as good a King as I can for Grinfields Town.'

The King listened to him attentively and he accepted his proposal, although he knew Edgar was older than his daughter. Nevertheless he worried only about the future of his kingdom, so if Edgar would assure the safety of Grinfields, it was enough — he wouldn't mind about his daughter.

The princess did not agree ... but the King didn't listen to her pleas. In the end, Hentmire explained to the King that she loved his servant. When the King heard these words, he got very, very angry and he objected to their love. Then the princess made a risky decision: they would elope to some isolated place where nobody could forbid their love.

When they were in the meadows, far away from the castle and close to the city walls, the King gave the order to capture and imprison them, until his daughter agreed to marry Edgar.

The castle guard went to look for them. One of the guards, who didn't understand the King's order properly, shot an arrow and the princess was mortally wounded. After a short period of time, her lover was so sad that he couldn't live any more.

When the King realised what had happened, he built a tomb and the princess and her servant were buried there. Nevertheless, the souls of Hentmire and her lover remained in the castle. The King died, the town of Grinfields was cursed and the castle was damned. But, Hentmire and Ronen could finally live together in love and peace.

The End

(Originally in Spanish)

A Magic Wand

Once upon a time my friend and
I saw a magician. We became
friends with him and he presented
us with a magic wand. Our first
wish was to make everyone
healthy. The second one was to
make everyone happy.
The third one was to make peace
all over the world. The next one
was to make everyone immortal.
Then we wished that everyone had
their own Cinderella at home. Then
suddenly, the wand just
disappeared.

We told everyone that we had
once had a magic wand, but no one
believed us.

(Originally in Russian)

69

Once upon a time, a long, long time ago, there were many witches and superheroes. One day a witch and a superhero met by mistake. They were both out doing good things for people. What they didn't know was that they were jealous of each other. Josephine the witch was jealous of Victoria because she could make people happy and make the world a better place. Victoria was jealous of the witch because she was able to look into the future and make people that are sick healthy. When they met, they began to argue about who was the best, but they were not allowed to use their magic. Without that, they did not know what to do. They just ended up staring at each other for three days and three nights. After a while, the witch Josephine said that it would be much better if they could put their magic powers together.

Victoria agreed and they went home and planned the following day's magic. The world was then turned into a much better place. When 100 years had gone by, the superhero Victoria died. The witch was used to having her around by then so after another two days and two nights she died as well. Now Victoria and Josephine are reunited in the land of heroes.

(Originally in Swedish)

71

The
Big
Mistake

'**Hear ye,** Hear ye,' the King orders, 'tonight is the night where we invite the poor and the lonely for dinner and forgive all of those sinners.' Later on that night the guests stampede through the vast open fields across the highest mountain and risk the slipperiest slopes. They finally arrive in the enormous giant monstrous castle where they eat and baffle and cackle. Through dawn and through dusk, they eat and talk until they are raided by two men with a hawk. One is fat, ugly and mean while the other stands there being frail but trying to act lean. They shout and roar and scare the visitors away and tell the King that now he must obey. The King walks away, ignoring them while they dance and sing like two stupid old men. Hip-hip hooray, they rejoice as the King joins a family, the poorest he had seen, in a house that was not much better than a box. He doesn't mind, he has never been happy, but now he is as snug as a bug in a rug and as happy as a baby in a nappy. Later on, those men got bored and fled the castle with a ship and a hoard. The King returned with his new-found friends and they laughed and had fun every day while enjoying the sun. **The End**

A long, long time ago lived a poor peasant called Tukasz who had an ill daughter and her name was Kinge. Tukasz was extremely poor and didn't have any money to buy medicines for his daughter. One day he went to the King and asked him for money. The King said 'no' and told him that he couldn't help all poor people. The peasant urged but the King was very mean and didn't change his mind. The peasant went back home. His daughter got a very high fever but he didn't have any medicine. He went to a neighbour and asked him for the money for medicine. The neighbour was happy to help Tukasz. Tukasz's neighbour protested against what the King had done. Instead of helping them, the King had imposed high taxes on poor people. The people banished the King from their country and they chose Tukasz as the new king. Everybody lived happily ever after.

(Originally in Polish)

75

Day Two

1 p.m.

The children are fresh from their first morning of separation from their former lives and have been canoeing on the lake, learning how to write and express themselves and working together on a camp newsletter using computers, or flying 75 yards at the speed of sound on a zipline (attached with a helmet and safety harness, of course) suspended between giant trees and over a small pond inhabited by the scary creatures of their night-time imagination.

At lunch, these young people, who have had to face their own mortality and be obedient to unresponsive adults in the midst of pain and sickness, can now reflect on a triumph of their mind and body in defying and conquering a challenge unimaginable to them days or weeks before. They can share or not, but they know they have done it.

While eating lunch, all these children, who even today are denied entry to 'normal' camps, can talk with others or just experience wearing their camp hats and T-shirts proudly. Being bald or missing a leg does not require an explanation or stares. As lunch ends, the CD player picks up a louder, syncopated beat of 1970s-era disco; a Cara or two start to role model a little silliness and group activity: Table two starts to pound their table slowly, building up to a crescendo, singing: 'We are table number two, we have spirit, so do you!' pointing to the next table away. And that gets repeated for twelve more tables and choruses. The Jordanian children still appear jet-lagged and seem a little culture shocked.

Then a spontaneous Conga line loops around the tables and benches and doubles up on itself, led by some of the previous years' veteran campers. The Jordanians look with interest, but hold back and resist, for now, their Cara's gentle urging to get up and shake a little bit. I suspect they will be full participants in a few days.

Totals

Total visits: 41 – 23 staff and 18 campers

Day Three

9.45 a.m.

The post-breakfast rush has started. The Medshed waiting room is crowded with fifteen people, mostly Caras. Camp policy is that if any child must be escorted anywhere, two adults must be present.

Connor is a 7-year-old who was brought in for his anti-haemophilia factor. Paulina places a local anaesthetic cream (EMLA), which looks like white toothpaste, over his upper chest. He has a tiny reservoir called a 'port' under the skin which has a tube connected through his veins to near the back chamber of his heart for intravenous infusions. This is because he has run out of veins in his arms and hands for getting injection treatments. He'll be back after the morning's lake-fishing activity time when the numbing will have taken effect.

A boy is in for the twice-daily foot soak for his infected ingrown toenail. This is a potential source of blood poisoning for children with cancer. The bacteria can get access to blood as the immune defences are compromised by the chemotherapy.

1 p.m.

The Jordanian boys and girls are really getting into the joining in and the spirit of competitive table banging with song at lunchtime. They have lost some inhibition; the girls got a kick out of seeing their Cara from Denmark beat the more athletic boys in hopping to the kitchen and being first back with the baked chicken and salads.

2.20 p.m.

One of the nurses comes back from the riding activity and is joyful. She was with a boy who has a brain tumour and has been wheelchair-bound for the last year with little upper-body strength. She was his 'side assistant', holding him up while he held the reins and went pony trekking for 20 minutes! Where else in the 'normal' camping world would this ever happen?

Totals

A light day today. Only 34 total visits are recorded, though it seems like more: 9 staff, 25 campers

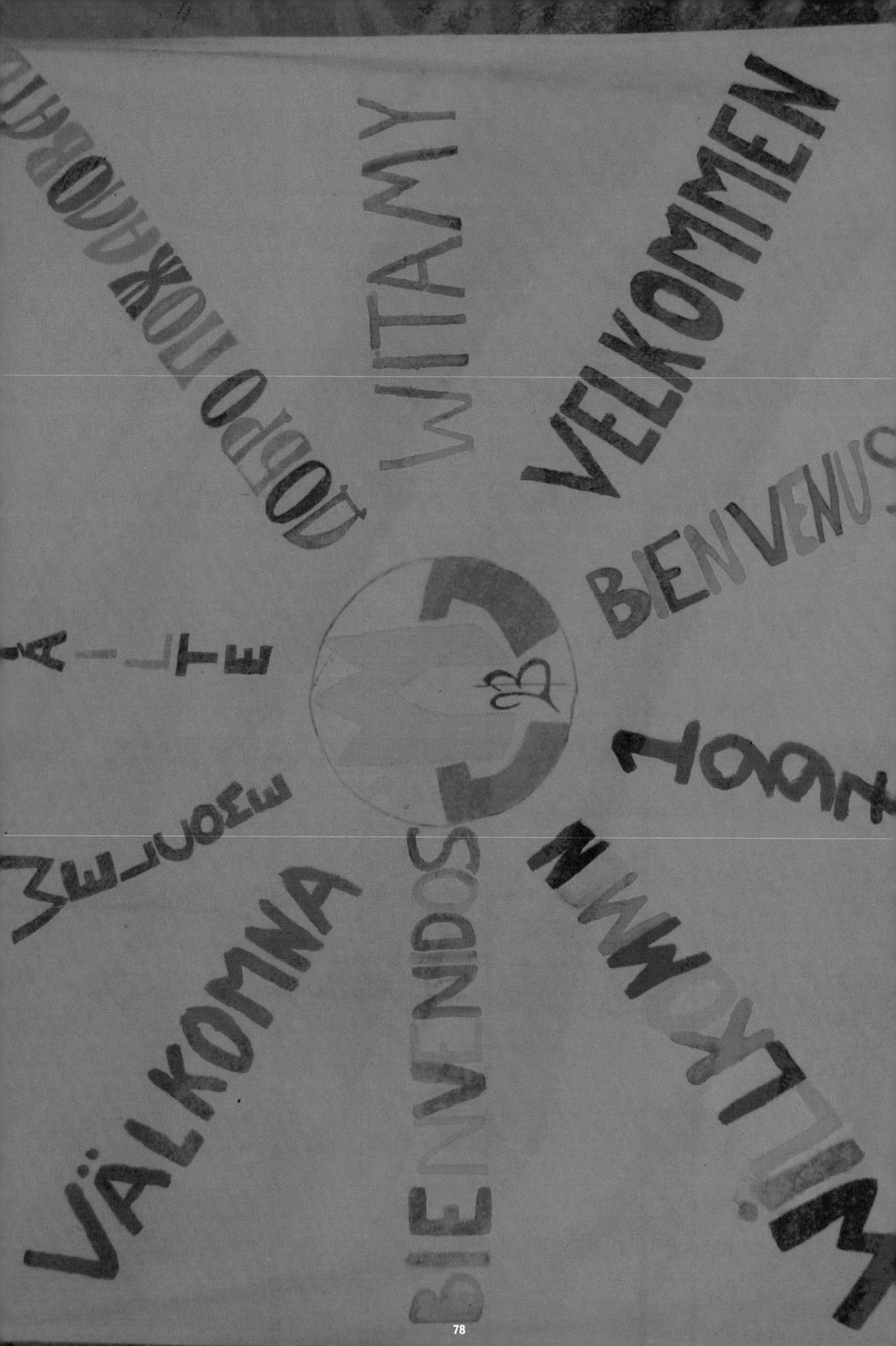

WITAMY

VELKOMMEN

ДОБРО ПОЖАЛОВАТЬ

BIENVENUS

VÄLKOMNA

BIENVENIDOS

WILLKOMMEN

Olympic Dreams

This year the Olympics are in Australia. I will compete in the 800 metres. It is two days to the competition and my stomach is full of butterflies. I really don't know. I am sitting on the plane wondering how it will end...

Suddenly my mobile phone is ringing. It's an Australian number. It starts with 100. It's the boss of the Olympics who tells me that last year's winner is sick. She has cancer in her leg and she has to have an amputation the day before the games begin. I become very sad and afraid, because now it could be cancelled. It's not so much that she's sick, but she was supposed to run with the Olympic flame ... I don't know what to say, so I tell the boss that he should call me later. I'm thinking and thinking...

Suddenly I remember that an old aunt of mine once ran with the flame. I call her up. She lifts the phone and says, 'Hello, this is Emilie.'

I say, 'Hello, it's me, Susann. It's a long time since we last talked to each other.'

'Yes, a very long time,' says Emilie.

'Well, I have a question,' I say. 'I have a problem. Last year's winner of the 800m in the Olympics has to have her leg amputated and we don't have anyone to run with the flame. So we thought that you could do it since you've done it before.' Emilie is quiet for a long time, but then she says 'OK'. She can meet at the course at 3 p.m.

I call the boss and say, 'Yes, I found someone who can do it!'

Now it's running day and I am really nervous about making a mistake and ending up last...

Three seconds to the start and I am running...

At the beginning, I was in third place, but in the last lap I'm leading! It's unbelievable ... 3 metres from the line, I fall. I've cut myself and am bleeding, but I know that I can't give up now, so I get up and run as fast as I can. I don't want to lose ... And I win!!!!

The whole audience stands and cheers for for me. I'm proud. I did it.

I became rich and famous. After that day, I became a girl with confidence and courage. I began to work with people who have been sick or are sick. I ran for people in wheelchairs and won a prize for it. Now my life is good and I am feeling great. I hope that the people I have helped are well. That was my goal in winning the 800 metres race at the Olympics.

(Originally in Norwegian)

I was sitting on the bleachers

I was excited, nervous...

My friend was just about to set a new world record in
 high jump.

It was time now. One minute left.

He starts clapping to get the audience going.

He runs. He makes it!

He's the best in the world.

I am so happy!

Olympic Games 2004

This year there is a new sport at the Olympic Games: canoeing!

At eight o' clock we began to get ready. First I put my wetsuit on. We always did canoeing with three people in the boat.

8.30 was the start!

It was 8.15 when we all had to go to the starting point. We sat down in the boats and waited for the starting signal. Our knees started to tremble, we were so excited.

The seconds seemed like hours, and we thought the starting signal would never come. We didn't hear the signal but suddenly everyone started canoeing.

When everyone else had already paddled very far in their canoes, we started. We thought it would be too late. We thought we would lose. But then we paddled as quickly as possible and we overtook all the other boats.

With a time of 2.8 minutes we were the fastest! More than a million people watched us. The crowds cheered and were happy with us.

We got a big gold medal, which was so heavy it wasn't possible to carry it on our own.

We celebrated with a big party that lasted the whole night!

(Originally in German)

OLYMPIC FEVER

PAUL IS SEVENTEEN years old. His favourite hobby is running marathons. He would like to train day and night, and so has been going to a sport university for two years.

His birthday is in a week. For a long time, he has wanted to take part in the Olympic Games.

The alarm clock is ringing. Today is Sunday — it's Paul's birthday. 'Finally I'm turning 18,' shouts Paul. His shouting wakens his room-mates. Their names are Marco and Phil.

'Don't shout like that. There are still people sleeping,' says Phil grumpily from under his duvet. Then the door opens and the head of the sports university comes in. He congratulates every pupil personally. 'Good morning!' shout the three boys in unison.

'You got a letter today. It seems to be quite important.' The manager goes away, smiling. Paul can't wait any longer and opens the envelope. There is a letter and a ticket. The letter says:

Dear Paul,

Happy birthday from your parents. We hope that you like the present. It is a ticket to the Olympic Games. But not only watching — oh no, it's a ticket to take part in the marathon.

Best wishes,

Mum and Dad

P.S. Best wishes also from Grandma and Grandpa and your brothers and sisters (they are all jealous about your present).

'Cool, I can take part in the Olympic Games,' shouts Paul.

'This can't be true,' says Marco.

'Yes it is!'

'You are lucky!'

Paul is a bit afraid when he looks out the window. Right now, he's sitting on a plane to Athens, where the Olympic Games are taking place. Two hours later, he arrives. He gets into his room in a hotel, changes his clothes and goes to the training area.

After a couple of days of training, it's the special day. With trembling knees, Paul is standing at the starting point. He hears the starting signal. Paul starts running like mad. But then he remembers that he has to save his strength for the end. He reduces speed and goes on running a bit more slowly. It's there; he can see the finish line, still running. Paul is in first  place. Suddenly his dream is over. For an instant, Paul's attention wanders and he slips. He tries to get back his balance, but it doesn't work and he falls down only a few centimetres from the finish line. Paul has to go to hospital because he is badly injured. And then comes the biggest shock for him: he is paralysed.

Paul can't believe it. His room-mates don't come to visit him at all. For them, Paul becomes a nobody. Because athletes need to be able to walk. That's what Marco and Phil think. But he doesn't want to give up yet. And he succeeds. Six weeks later, Paul can go home from hospital.

4 years later...
There's the starting signal. The athletes start running. In first place, there is the 22-year-old Paul Newton, after him there is Phil Marston and Marco Graham. And Paul Newton wins the Olympic Games marathon.

(Originally in German)

Day Four

7.30 a.m.

Go for a jog around the castle grounds. Dispense some hot water and add a tea bag in the castle kitchen for some hydration. Lying around the kitchen are seven trays of baked chocolate-chip cookies and cookies of dough and Rolo chocolate caramel (my carbohydrate indulgence and weakness) mixed by the younger campers from Cottage 7. They also seem to contain some mystery contents. I had better avoid…

10.15 a.m.

A boy from England needs a blood count, since he has been non-compliant at home, and at camp is actually receiving his chemotherapy under the watchful eyes of the nurses. His oncologist wants the blood count to make sure he does not get toxic. I try what should be a routine venapuncture and miss on the first pass. He is not angry and seems resigned that I will need to try the other arm.

   I see a vein over his left wrist and attempt a second time. The needle stick is true and we draw the blood that I will take into Dublin's children's hospital — the facility runs all our blood studies for children at camp.

10.45 a.m.

A boy comes in with two Caras, each with orange war paint on their nose and cheeks, à la Mel Gibson in *Braveheart* (they needed a cottage bonding experience). He is here because the gauze dressing covering his access port is loose. It is flapping in the breeze and Eimear takes him in and redresses it with stronger tape. Back to canoeing.

11 a.m.

The nurses are in the pharmacy room, as they are every day at this time, reading over the medication orders and placing the over 125 medications for lunchtime distribution in small plastic bags that will be given to the appropriate child at his or her cottage table in the dining hall.

A hand-scrawled note is tossed through the doorway by a masked child; it tells us that the seven large cuddly dwarfs who usually rest on the waiting-room couch have been kidnapped, and if we want ever to see them again we must provide chocolate, fizzy drinks and chips as ransom. We are not sure how to respond — as we have been unsure for the past nine years of doll kidnaps. Cora voices her indignation that such a cheesy note requests such a large ransom. She tells a masked cottage kidnapper that we expect a far more sophisticated note with artwork and legible printing. The pressure mounts…

3.30 p.m.
A nurse comes into the Medshed in an ecstatic mood, soon followed by the smiling boy who was fresh from his triumph of horseback riding yesterday. Today, he conquered the high-ropes course, being suspended 35 feet up and traversing the logs, attached by ropes, pulleys and harness. The nurse brings him to one of the resting rooms and tucks him in for an hour's nap.

This child has been wheelchair bound for the past year due to a complication called posterior fossa syndrome or cerebellar mutism. When the brain tumour is removed, certain functions controlled by the back area of the brain start to fail, and rehabilitation for voice, swallowing and upper-body strength can take years for recovery.

9.30 p.m.
Nurses' rounds. The Italian boys in Cottage 8 are in bed and greet Paulina with a 'Hello Paulina' in perfect English. They take their chemo medications without a stir and wish her a *'Bono sera'* on leaving.

Another cottage is another story. One boy claims that he can take only one pill at a time, each separated by five minutes. So Paulina returns four times and he tells her she can come back to put on the cream later. Paulina leaves the tube with him.

It is so interesting to me how different parental responses can be to catastrophic illness. Some are able to recover their role as parents and put normal limits on their children's behaviour. Others are so glad their child is alive that little restrictions or differentiation occur about acceptable versus unacceptable behaviour. Our job here at camp is to provide a safe environment and provide choices and alternatives.

Totals
Total Medshed visits: 29 — 5 staff and 24 campers

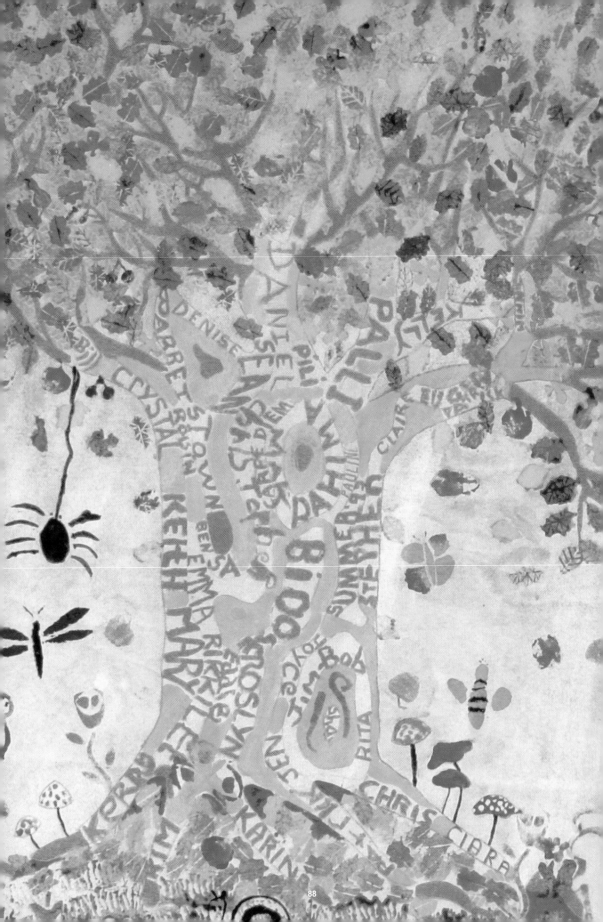

The Nature Room

First it was a seed.

Then it started to grow
bigger into a rose.

And then I picked it up.

The rose would be kind
but also tough and able
to defend itself.

It would be very innocent
and sweet.

A rose in the garden
stands so innocent and
sweet.

I saw it when I passed by.

It stood in the sun and
enjoyed itself.

I picked it up to bring it
home.

(Originally in Swedish)

I'm the yellow flower.
In spring I'm a little baby.
When the summer is coming
I'm a grown-up flower
And people pass by and look at me and
  say I'm Beautiful.
But when the autumn is near
I will be old and my leaves
Will turn brown, and in the end fall off.

The grass is greener
But the trees are cleaner
And the sky is blue

I'm an apple.

Every summer little purple flowers grow out
here and there

And later it turned out to be me,

An apple,

Green and fresh,

Just hanging there on the tree all day long,

The wind grabs the little leaves around me
and makes them sing,

I love it,

Just hanging there, listening to the wind
singing in my leaves,

That's what I call life.

As the flowers silently sway away in
    the gentle breeze,
They come to dance,
Vibrant colours fill the summer skies,
Their delicate wings flutter like silken
    petals shimmering in the sun.
As autumn falls so do they,
And the once lovely pictures of
    perfection
Are now at peace with the world.

It began when I was a small flower waiting for someone. Suddenly one day I heard a terrible sound. It came closer and closer, and it also became louder and louder, until a big bee came by and stuck something in me.

Then one day I began to lose my leaves and I became a round ball, who said 'Goodbye' to my mother and left. When I found a suitable place, I began to grow.

As I developed over a long time, I became bigger and bigger, until finally I looked like my mother. I grew a lot of flowers and I hope they will all do well.

(Originally in Norwegian)

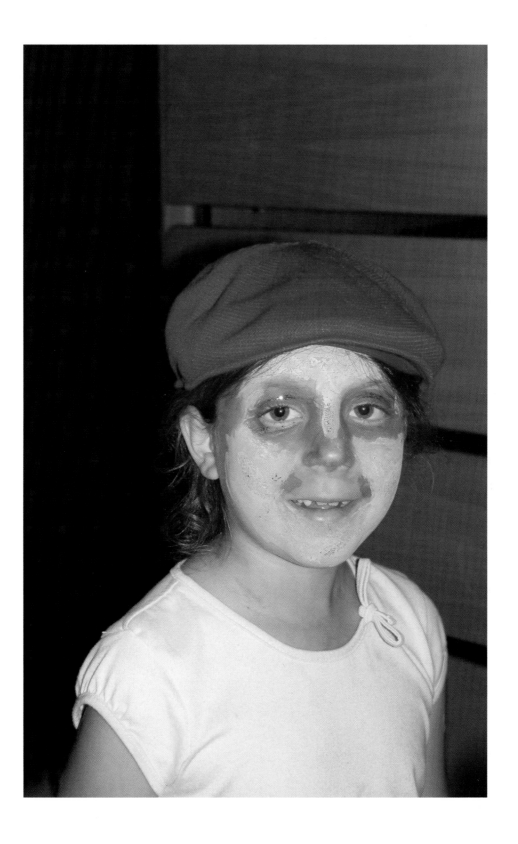

I am a flower
That blossoms in the day time
Everyone adores me
Because I am beautiful
People say nice things
About me
They say I am nice, friendly, caring and
Always show love towards others.
That means I am love and friendship
I am also coloured red signifying passion
People can identify me from far away
Because of my colour

A leaf

It starts as a little bud hanging on a tree looking on those who pass by.

It grows bigger and bigger.

Some day when it's fall or winter, it falls down and just lies right there on the ground.

(Originally in Norwegian)

The wind blew a tiny seed,
Into the shade of a rose tree,
The little seed said, " I wish I was as pretty as you.'
The rose tree replied, ' See that tree, it does too.'
Two years passed without a word,
Until the sound of digging was heard.
The plant that was once the seed
Looked down as the man completed the deed.
It said, ' All things must come to an end,
Even your beauty, my friend.'
Now people look at the plant and smile,
I guess the wait was worthwhile.

The Flower Bud

She lives in a big garden and around her are apple trees. She has lots of friends and relations.

The bud is red, orange and round.

At her stalk she has many little thorns. Later she will become a beautiful, purple-coloured flower.

But at the moment she is still a bud, so she is not standing in focus, she is closed and shy.

(Originally in German)

Rainbow flowers through
Sun shining in the sky blue
With bees buzzing too

The sun is shining
The roses are all colours
The garden is nice.

Found a flower in the garden
How would I describe it?
It smells like summer, sweet and free,
It looks sensible, secrety and also open,
It feels so velvety and rough,
It is yellow like the sun.
It's green like an emerald,
And pink which is beyond definition!
This is the flower which I mean!

Daisy, Daisy

I'm a little daisy.
Some call me crazy.
Some think I'm nasty.
Some think I'm nice.
If you think I'm nasty,
What about last night's rice?

I grow from a seed.
I get called a little weed.
I stand up tall and try
To face the sun.
If I grew in India,
I could become a bun.

I open when I can.
I'm a little flower with a suntan.
I'm up in the spring,
Up in the summer,
But when winter comes,
It's such a major bummer.

I open my steeples,
And then turn my petals.
I wait for little bugs
That move as fast as slugs.
I need the pollen from other plants.
If I don't get it,
I haven't a chance.
Once I reproduce, I've had it,
I'm cut loose.

Day Five

9 a.m.

Morning visits are for the Italian boys to self-infuse anti-haemophiliac factor.

Another boy has never self-infused before and Luca thinks he is ready. He is not on prevention doses, but he does have pain in his target place, the right knee, which means that a bleed has started and will not abate without Factor 9 to stop it. After preparing the syringes, diluting the factor with water and pulling it out into the syringe, he is ready. He feels for the veins in the crook of his left arm for what must be 15 minutes. Luca places the needle in his right hand and the boy needs to feel the veins again all over. Finally, with his friend watching, the boy inserts the needle into the skin and pulls back with an 'ouch'. 'It was like an electric shock,' he says in Italian. Then he tries again and that's it! A direct hit and blood comes back in the thin tube almost to the end cap. Luca attaches the syringe and the boy starts to push… Magic! Then he realises he has been holding his breath for 45 seconds, inhales, and looks a little faint. He breathes rapidly and in two minutes the job is done. Another triumph. On the other side of the room, a Cara is also self-infusing his Factor. He was here as a camper seven years ago and now is a Cara, a role model, and a university student. He tells the boys: 'Haemophilia didn't stop me.'

A girl is here for a dressing change. She is 9 years old but as tall as a 3-year-old, because chronic kidney disease has stunted her growth. She was part of a new-age dance troupe entertainment at breakfast and scraped her knee on a turn. It is also a handy time to change the dressing on her venous access used for her dialysis.

Totals

A busy day: 43 – 5 staff and 38 campers

Day Six

2.45 p.m.

It is interesting to me that so many Caras have had serious health issues. One way of coping and honouring health is to give back by working so diligently and with such energy with the special children who come to Barretstown. It was Florence Nightingale, an English nurse, who in the Crimean war said: 'It is better to light a candle than curse the darkness.' The Caras project light into darkened places.

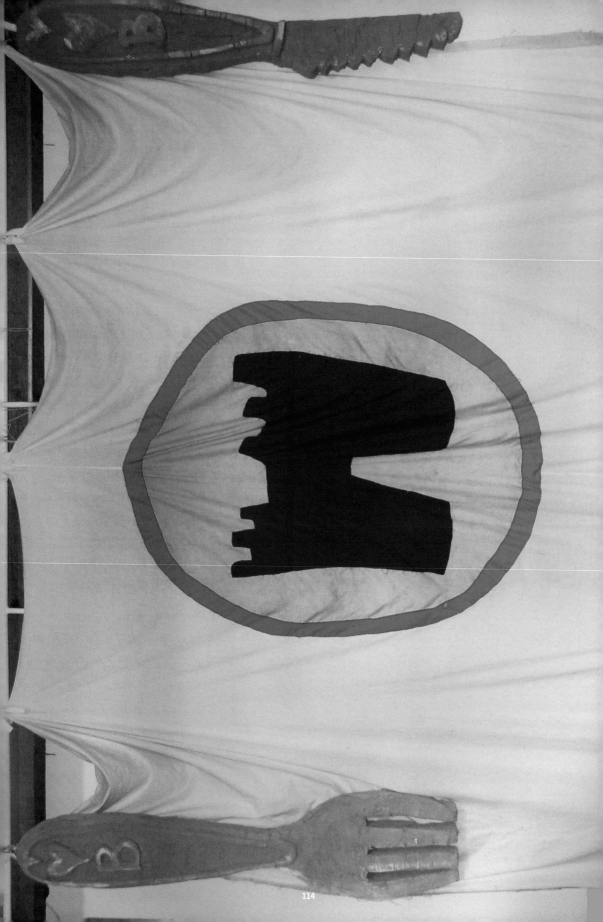

Here's
a Funny
Story...

Meow! Kristen woke up early to the smell of rotting meat. 'Eww,' he uttered. Kristen lived in a trashcan, not by choice of course. He thought that today he would look for someone to be friends with. 'ROAR!!!' roared someone in the bushes. 'Meow!' uttered Kristen, startled. It was a lion. 'Meow', 'ROAR!' Kristen wanted to run away but he couldn't get out of the trashcan. 'I've got something on my back and I can't reach it!' wailed the lion.

'I could,' said Kristen in a very small voice. And so Kristen pulled off the startled zookeeper, housewife and computer salesperson with his teeth, then the two members of the cat family became friends.

'I escaped from the city zoo two days ago and those people's continuous screaming has given me a throbbing headache,' said the lion. So even though it was still early afternoon, the lion went to sleep.

'Uh, oh!' said Kristen in a very small voice when he saw the rustling leaves in the bushes. 'Here little lion, here.' It was men from the zoo coming for their lion.

'No!' shouted Kirsten although you and me would hear, 'Meow meow!'

Unfortunately Ferdinand, the lion-catcher who was hoping for a promotion from his current job at the zoo, mucking out the elephant cage, heard him meowing and headed hurriedly in that direction. 'Aww look, Frank, a cute little kitty! I'm sure we could have him at the petting zoo!'

Uh, oh, Kristen was found. 'Meow, no wait roar, no roar, no, I've got it ROAR!!!'

'Ah no, this kitten is possessed!! I'm out of here!'

So Kristen and the lion were friends from then on and Ferdinand was left to live out the rest of his days in a one-man apartment mucking out elephant poop.

The Sloth that Wasn't Lazy

Once upon a time, there was a sloth that wasn't like any other sloth. He didn't hang out on trees, but instead went out playing with his friend, Pepe the Parrot. His name was Tilmann. One day he was standing in front of a huge river. He wanted to jump right in, but the other sloths called out, 'You'll die if you do that!'

Tilmann called back, 'No, I won't. You're just too lazy, so follow me!' Finally, he jumped … and the river's current took him right out. The other sloths jumped up, forgot that they were lazy, called their friend Pepe the Parrot and asked for his help. Pepe said that he could help a little, but the sloths had to do the main part.

'All right, but what should we do?' they asked.

'Come here and I will whisper it to you. The other animals are not allowed to hear it,' Pepe said.

They met in a group and, afterwards, ten of them prepared big posters, two got benches and tables, four sloths got some food and Pepe went looking for Tilmann. He found him! He was right in front of the waterfall. Pepe threw a rope and said, 'Hold on tight. Help is on its way.' Ten minutes later, the other sloths appeared and started to prepare everything. Tilman watched and suddenly the other animals arrived too. Elephant, lion, tiger and antelope came over, because it was a party. The lion didn't eat any of the others, the tiger either, as he had become a vegetarian about a month before the party. So nobody was scared. Everybody was standing on one side of the river. Tilmann called out, 'I want to get out of the river. Have you forgotten about me?'

'No, of course not!' The elephant and the lion made a bet on who would be the first to get Tilmann out. The elephant won and everybody partied. And since then, there isn't a lazy sloth to be found

(Originally in German)

119

There once was a monkey called Denise who hated when she had to climb trees.

'What's wrong?' asked Paul. She said nothing at all. 'So why don't you want to climb trees?'

By the time she explained her reason it was almost Christmas season, because she had so many reasons to tell. It's because of the wind, the snake and that awful smell.

So Paul went to the shop and bought a lovely shirt, an umbrella, snake killer and a deodorant can. Paul said, 'Now you will get a nice tan.'

Paul went up the tree and killed the snake and sprayed the deodorant can, then set up the umbrella where the wind could not get it and you'd never get wet. So Paul said to Denise, 'Now you can climb trees!' and Denise jumped with joy.

There once was a farmer. He bought a new piece of land. But he had to divide it because he had a wild bull. One half was for the bull, the other half was for the farmer. One day ten cows said to Hooktail, the bull: 'Hooktail, you'll never manage to jump over the fence.' So Hooktail went back a few yards, ran at the fence and jumped it. He said, 'Well, what do you say now?' And then the cows said, 'B…Bu…But Hook.' The bull asked them, 'Why did you call me Hook?'

The cows answered, 'Because your tail is still hanging on the fence!'

The Upside-down Story

I live on meatball street number pork three floors on the bottom. I was lying in my bottomless bed reading interesting phone-books. Suddenly I heard soundless steps in the stairs. A man came in with a knife without a blade. He stabbed it in my heart but luckily I had my heart in my mouth. I ran to the beach, jumped on to the bridge and sailed away. After a long journey of five seconds I capsized and floated into land on a rusty nail. I was on a desert island where naked cannibals were dancing around with their hands in their back pockets. I went to a cabin and kicked the door open and jumped inside through the window. Inside I saw five sandwiches that were already eaten and then I ate them. After that, I went into the jungle. There I was face to face with two big lions. I shot one of them with my last bullet. After that I started to lift cotton until I was in pain. With that shot of pain I shot the second lion. I then started to walk further into the jungle where I fell into a trap containing a loose tiger. My life was hanging on a thread and on that thread I climbed up. I ran to the beach where I screamed until I heard an echo and sailed home.

Non-sequitur

Once upon a time, there was a castle named Barretstown. The castle was very big; it was also haunted. We do lots of activities. We all live in a cottage village. There are dragons and poison snakes in the castle. There is a moat around the castle, and there are sea monsters. The owners of the castle were very vicious and their names were 'Vicious Vicky' and 'Vicious Victor'. In the tower of the castle was Dracula and werewolves. And there was a mattress to jump on. The cottages have slime and spiders. And nobody can sleep in there any more — so they went camping. There were two superheroes, 'Guy with Light bulb' and 'Guy with Jackhammer'. And there was Frankenstein, a scorpion and the king of the underworld. His sister is there and she is really disgusting and really good at playing the piano. And there is an alien protector. 'Guy with Light bulb' melts the villains and the 'Guy with Jackhammer' buries them. And by the piano people were dancing.

(Originally in Icelandic)

A Barretstown Tale

ONE SUNNY SUMMER'S DAY in a strange land called Barretstown, Declan and Pig went to visit Alli in Cottage 9. On the way they visited Cottage 7 to invite them all to a party in Cottage 9. 'I don't know,' said Pig, 'as I go to bed very early every night.'

'But it's Alli's birthday party,' said Declan. 'It's going to be a big surprise for her.'

Pig said, 'OK, maybe I can risk one night.'

There was a band playing at the party—they were going to sing the 'Cha cha slide'. Declan and Pig wanted to delay Alli, so that they could get the cottage ready for the party. Declan and Pig knew that Quinn secretly fancied Alli because they were friends in high school. So Declan and Pig went to Quinn to ask him to make the cake so he could dance with Alli. Quinn was more than happy to accept. Quinn's cake had fairy liquid, fish and eggshells in it and it included shoe polish to make it look like a chocolate cake. While the rest were preparing the party, Alli got a call from her boss saying that she had a meeting in Barretstown's Creation Station. While getting ready, Alli heard a knock on the door and quickly put her jacket on and ran downstairs to open the door. Kerry was at the door to bring her to the meeting. Kerry's car broke down in the middle of the road so they had to walk to the meeting. Along the way they met the band and asked them what were they doing there. They were going to a huge party in Cottage 9 and Alli's phone rang, it was her boss saying the meeting was cancelled. They asked the band if they could ride to the party with them. The band said of course they could. So they went to the party.

Quinn danced with Alli at the party. But the real Alli ran in the door, to see them dancing. So who was Quinn really dancing with? Declan. Quinn took off the wig to see who he was really dancing with. He rubbed his hands against the fake Alli's face so that he could see it was his good friend Declan, and Declan laughed at him and told him it was a prank.

Day Seven

10 a.m.
Luca brings in his boys for their assembly line of Anti-haemophiliac Factor therapy. As usual, it goes without a hitch.

2 p.m.
I walk out on the flint-based trail and then, as I pass by the 'low ropes' course, the outline of the 40-foot-tall beams and log cross bars of the 'high ropes' becomes visible through the tall trees.

   The low-ropes course demands that the children cooperate and work as a team (with word and sign directions) to accomplish tasks such as crossing a 7-foot-wide stream, or passing through a rope spider web without touching the ropes outlining the holes. In contrast, the high-ropes course is an individual challenge to diminish fear of heights, while balancing on beams 20 and 40 feet above the ground.

2.30 p.m.
Watching the Caras instruct the children about the safety harness, ropes, pulleys, links and helmets before attempting the climb always is a marvel to me. Each child knows that this is a challenge to be conquered and is aware of both danger and his or her own fears.

   They all listen intently to the Cara who holds the rope which suspends them through a series of pulleys and is responsible for their safety.

   A 10-year-old is watchful of his comrades who precede him, watching for clues as to how they use the rope, and climb up the first 10 feet against the pole, pulling themselves up, ring-by-ring. Now it is his turn, and he pulls himself up to the first level and steadies himself, before crossing on the 30-foot-long beam, grabbing on each of the successive eight hanging ropes for balance. Words of encouragement come from below in Spanish and Irish-accented English.

   The Cara pulls on the rope lifting him 10 more feet into the air and finally he is on the highest tightrope. Now he must traverse 30 feet back to the vertical beam before he will either climb down or ask the Cara to let him jump in mid-air and descend on rope and pulley for an exciting, flying landing. This boy chooses the flying leap. One of his cottage room-mates joins him on the ground and hands him his crutches, as they walk off to the bench together. The boy had his left leg amputated last year and completed chemotherapy for his osteogenic sarcoma. He is a survivor and victor of cancer … and the high ropes.

7 p.m.

There will probably be few visits in the next hour or two, as all the children are getting ready for disco night. Even the younger boys take a bath or shower in preparation for this night's events.

7.30 p.m.

There are 20 limousines, everything from six-door stretch Mercedes to Rover town cars, lining the driveway up to the castle, ready to transport three to six children and a Cara or two around the castle grounds, onto the street and back again through the entry gates, finally leaving the children off in front of the all-purpose theatre (disco) which will host tonight's event.

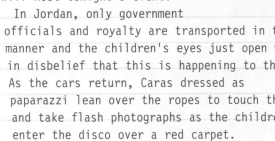

In Jordan, only government officials and royalty are transported in this manner and the children's eyes just open wide in disbelief that this is happening to them. As the cars return, Caras dressed as paparazzi lean over the ropes to touch them and take flash photographs as the children enter the disco over a red carpet.

9.10 p.m.

Maria, my physician partner, is dancing with the Spanish girls. The high-ropes boy is dancing with his Caras, executing a 360-degree spin with the help of his crutches, and continues the dance as he moves over to another group of boys and girls. This is my yearly fix that reaffirms how valuable this camp is for these children.

Totals

Total visits today: 53 — 7 staff and 66 campers

SUMMER 2004
SESSION 3

'Freddy — The Frog who Couldn't Quack' and Other Animal Tales

In the future, people will really love animals. In order to live with them in the huge forests, people must take care of animals and animals must take care of people.

This forest was near North America. There were about twelve species of birds and about seventeen horses. There were fewer people than animals, but they tried to take care of them and feed them as best as they could. One of the horses was the tallest and fastest. He was white and stood out from the others. The people had a chief called Animal Friend. He became a chief because he was the one who brought the animals.

The place where the animals lived was green with prairies and you could smell the flowers.

The relationship between people and animals was very good. And they lived happily ever after.

(Originally in Greek)

My name is Sarah the pony and this

is the story of my life. My favourite things are humans, and food. I lie in a stable all the time, sitting, watching the world go by. My hay is warm and fuzzy also with food spread all around me. I have been ridden on so many times. I am going to tell you about one time which was my favourite time EVER!!!

Sally's hands and legs were so soft and tender I really enjoyed it. She rode me so carefully and skilfully I didn't have to think about whether she was going to fall. I just wish the person who rides me now would do the same thing that Sally did.

At night I stand upright and watch the shining stars shine! I really enjoy that but not as much as being ridden on. Anyway, that is the story of my life.

Freddy –
The Frog who
Couldn't Quack

Once upon a time, there lived a frog named Freddy, who had a very big problem. He couldn't quack.

So he went to see a speech therapist, but the hospital was very far from his house.

On the way, he met a stork whose name was Hugo. Hugo's family didn't like him and sent him away because he was a vegetarian and didn't want to eat frogs. The stork was very sad because of it and he began to drink. It was the reason why he spent all his money.

When he met Freddy, he was very sad and because he drank alcohol most of the time, instead of seeing one frog, he saw two!!

Being so depressed, he decided to go for it and eat them. However, when he accidentally hit Freddy with his beak, the poor little froggy went, 'ribbit ribbit'. He was so happy to be able to make a real frog sound that he gave Hugo all his money. Hugo quitted drinking, found himself a job and they were best friends ever after.

A Day in the Life of a Puppy

I was woken up today by some noisy customers poking and prodding me and the other four puppies that I live with in Petunia's Pet Store. Our pen is next to a cats' pen and they always provoke us and then we get into a fight and we get into trouble.

Anyway, the customers didn't buy us in the end and I couldn't go back to sleep so I decided to go over and have some breakfast.

For the rest of the day, I ended up being hissed at by cats, yawning, chasing my tail and watching traffic. Then I went back to sleep and was woken up the next day the same way.

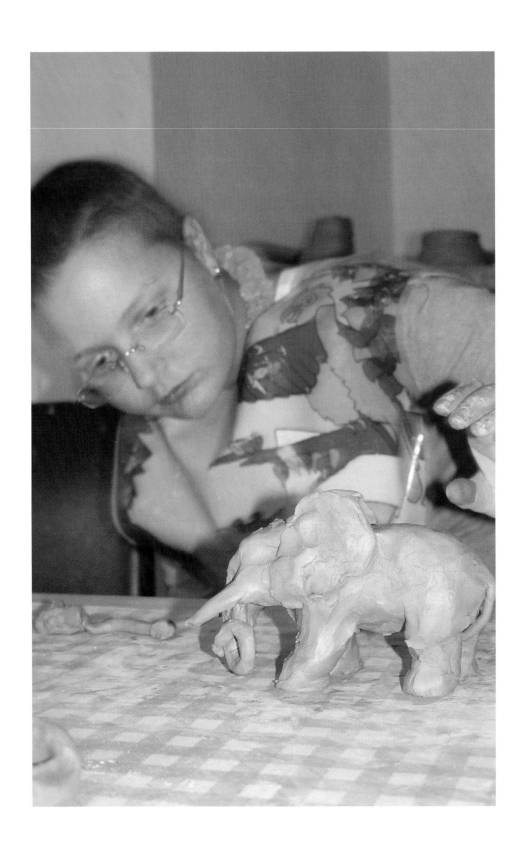

Life

I'm a snake and I live in the jungle. I sleep between rocks and love to eat mice. You probably want to know who my enemies are. I don't like predators, except the lion and the tiger. They are my friends.

One summer's day, I woke up and looked right into the eyes of an elephant. I was scared, but he said, 'Don't be scared. I'm not a bad person.' I turned around and went back to sleep.

Everybody says that I'm dangerous, but that's not true. Lots of children are afraid of me, but to be honest, I'm more afraid of them. If you want to come and visit me, look for me underneath the leaves. I'm not up in the trees. Pepe is a parrot. I got to know him on a holiday some time ago, when we stayed in a hotel which was inside a hollow log. Tilmann is a sloth and I also got to know him during holidays. We had lots of fun, but Pepe left before us. He didn't get his favourite kind of worms there, so he left. Tilmann and I stayed longer.

Bye bye, see you later.
Your snake

(Originally in German)

The Little Oyster

Once there was a little ugly oyster. It lay at the bottom of a large ocean. Every night the oyster looked at the lovely moon and wished to be lovely.

One day, a beautiful fish came to the oyster and said, "Am I not beautiful?" "Yes," said the oyster, "you are really beautiful." The fish disappeared.

After a little while, a fisherman came fishing near the oyster. He threw in his net. When he came home, he found many fish caught in the net he dragged in. At the bottom lay the ugly oyster. The fish were then cleaned and sold on the very same evening. The oyster was so ugly that the fisherman threw him back into the ocean. But what nobody knew was that inside the oyster lay a beautiful pearl.

To this day, the oyster is still in the ocean and gets to gaze at the moon.

(Originally in German)

Once upon a time, a boy and a girl were exploring the Barretstown jungle. Suddenly, a monkey came to tell them that there was a lion who was wounded. They followed the monkey and they saw that the lion's tail was injured. The jungle had a lot of plants, the air was warm and wet. There were waterfalls and a river and many animals hidden in trees. The monkey was big and hairy. He was very noisy and naughty. The boy and the girl were brother and sister who lived in an abandoned cottage in the middle of the jungle next to the river. The lion was big and had beautiful fur. He was very brave, but as he was wounded, he was very afraid. The monkey, despite being afraid of the lion, had been rescued once by him from evil hunters and was in his debt, so he called the rest of the kids.

The lion was used to having to protect himself from hunters and when he saw the kids, he thought they were evil. When the lion was about to attack, the monkey got in the middle to protect the kids from the lion and explained to him that

they were friends. The lion realised that they were friends because the monkey defended them and showed them his wounded tail. The kids took the lion to their cottage and looked for healing plants that had blue flowers and red thorns.

The following day, the lion was cured and was eternally grateful to the kids. As a reward, he gave them a tour through the jungle to help them with their search. They became friends forever and had many other adventures together.

(Originally in Spanish)

It was a bad day for B.J. the snake making traps. Bradley the lion, who was out for a walk, got trapped in one of the snake's traps. Bradley began to shout as loud as he could. The kangaroo and the dog came to the rescue of the lion. Bradley the lion screamed, 'Get me down!' The dog and kangaroo eventually got him down by biting the ropes. They all went in search of the snake who was hiding in the trees just a short distance from where they were. When they found B.J. the snake, they asked him, 'Why are you setting traps for us to fall into?'

B.J the snake responded by saying that he was simply trying to catch some food. The lion and the kangaroo said, 'You should make smaller traps.' The snake said, 'Good idea,' and apologised for any pain that he might have caused the lion.

The White Mare

Once upon a time, there was a young white mare. Her name was Maria. She went out for a walk in a green and lush pasture and there she found her three friends accompanied by a goat with a purse hanging from one of its horns. They came up to Maria and the goat offered her some violet-coloured bottles. Maria opened a bottle of flies and they flew directly into her blue eyes. The goat then threw a drop of liquid onto Maria's head and the flies flew away, terrified.

(Originally in Spanish)

The Horse

Once upon a time, there was a horse that lived at a camp. The camp's name is Barretstown. The horse can run with his friends, and eat in the big fields... The bad thing for him is that lots of kids get on top of him and he has to run, so lots of kids hurt him. He can't complain because no one understands him. Well, we humans can understand some of the things that he tells us by his gestures, but I don't understand him too well because I don't spend a lot of time with him. What I think is great is that Barretstown has given him and many other horses a huge field, and it gives them proper food like hay, etc, and in the winter time, when the camp is closed, they're also taken care of. Here in Ireland, as it rains a lot, often they just have to get into their stables which are quite dark, and that's really the worst thing for them when it rains. I still haven't gone horse riding at Barretstown but today I'm waiting for it very anxiously because it's a beautiful animal and I won't hurt him at all. I love everything except for their poos because they're big and smell really bad.

(Originally in Spanish)

Rajá, the Great

Once upon a time, there was a tiger called Rajá who was very fast and fierce. Everyone was scared of him, even in the North Pole. Rajá lived in India. He was different from the rest and the prettiest in the whole tiger herd. He was striped and had a white spot that looked very good on him.

   Once he was going for a walk when he heard a bark and he said, 'That must be a dog!' Rajá tried to bark, but he couldn't do it. He went back to the tiger herd and no one liked him. He decided never to go back and never to kill again. He did that and the whole herd wanted to be his friend and that is how he became known as Rajá, the Great!

(Originally in Spanish)

Drago the Dragon

Hello, my name is Drago. I am a dragon. I am 4 metres tall and I can spit flames. I am going to tell you a story about myself.

Once upon a time, I went into the jungle and searched for my friends, but I couldn't find them. So I asked my friend the squirrel and he said, 'Leo the bad guy has kidnapped them!'

I said, 'What?'

The squirrel answered, 'Your friends are in the Cave of Death.'

'OK, let's go, what are we waiting for?'

'I am going to tell you about Leo the lion. He is really bad, mean, nasty and strong.'

So we walked quickly to the cave. Suddenly, we heard their voices out of a labyrinth. 'Oh no, a labyrinth. How will we find them?'

'I know, the squirrel will walk along the walls and if he finds Leo, then he should come back.' And the squirrel returned after some time and showed me the way. Suddenly we heard Leo the lion, so I had no choice, I had to fight him. He attacked me and we fought bitterly, but I could beat him with the help of my flames. I surprised him and he fell into a valley. I rescued my friends and we flew into our volcano.

(Originally in German)

HORSE RIDING

FIRST WE HAD TO BRUSH THE HORSES

and then a lady put the saddle on. Then we put the helmets on our heads. Then we took the horses to a field. When we took them to the field, we had to climb on the horses but I was on crutches so the lady took me to a stair thing. Then I had to do the splits to climb the horse. The horse was so high. When I climbed on the horse, the lady had to fix my seat and put my legs in the iron things at the side of the horse. She took me to the field again and John had to do the same thing as I did. John came back and the lady started to talk about how to hold the horse and everything. Tina was holding my horse and John was holding Thomas's horse. So we started walking and we had to turn the horses around and we had to stop them.

After that, the lady told us how to make the horses go fast and after that we learned really well how to ride a horse. So then she took us down the field for a walk with the horse. The lady had a dog named Charlie and it barked at my horse. My horse was scared and it started to run on its own. Then the horse turned around and I nearly fell off and Tina calmed the horse down but that didn't help so the owner of the horses went to the horse and held onto the lead. After that I was a little scared of the horse but I know it was the dog. Then the lady took the dog inside and the horse calmed down. So then I had to get off the horse and I did another splits coming off.

I really enjoyed horse riding.

Day Eight

10.20 a.m.

The boy with a sore knuckle yesterday has tenderness all along his first metacarpal bone behind the finger. He needs an X-ray, as he has had two leg fractures the previous year. He is in his second year of leukaemia therapy and many children lose calcium in their bones and fracture more easily. We need to send him to the hospital in Dublin, so arrangements need to be made for one of the nurses to accompany him and a driver to take him there.

11.20 a.m.

Our frequent visitor comes back complaining of pain where I injected his Factor earlier. There is no swelling and he settles for a Tylenol, if he goes back to meet his group. This makes 21 visits so far this session. He is going for a record for the most 'unsick' visits.

2.10 p.m.

A little 8-year-old girl from Dublin has vomited once again today and wants to lie down for a while. Her Cara from Scotland keeps her company while we get a small TV and a tape of *The Little Princess* for her to watch in one of the comfy rooms. She had a PNET brain tumour and completed her radiation and chemotherapy six months ago. These children can vomit for no reason for years afterward, but it can also mean a tumour recurrence. Our job is to make her comfortable in camp and let her primary doctors figure that one out. She looks emaciated though, and we will draw attention to her poor nutrition in our letter to her doctors at the end of camp.

5.10 p.m.

The hospital calls as well as the Senior Registrar. They give the blood-count results as well as the modifications we must make in the doses of anti-leukaemia medications for five children.

5.30 p.m.

A nurse is busy writing the doctors' letters about children who have had blood counts or major events. She has prepared the names of five campers who need letters. So far, these are all Irish children and all are taken care of by one physician in Dublin. With her help, it takes only about 20 minutes to get them completed. It is a custom of the camp to give this feedback as it establishes and maintains a good relationship with the referring physicians.

6 p.m.

There is a palpable excitement about this evening's programme.

  The camp talent show also provides me with a different prism to view each child. When they come in to have blood drawn or an anti-haemophiliac injection, they are my camp patients and I am concentrating on their veins. I sometimes forget to see them in the environment of normal childhood with their unique skills.

7.40 p.m.

First, each act is introduced by two Caras in outrageous costumes with cloaks, one sporting giant butterfly wings and bright make-up. Then each act is translated into Spanish, Arabic, Italian and Greek by the translators, attired in royal court costumes of the Middle Ages.
The acts are presented by the cottages and may be solos and/or groups. For many of the children, the non-verbal urgency to perform is to demonstrate 'I am here and I am alive', 'My cancer does not define or subsume me.' They may be bald or emaciated, wear wigs or costumes they have designed; but each one's performance makes a loud statement about what truly constitutes heroism.

  One and one half hours ago, this boy on stage was a weak, tired-looking, vulnerable child, asleep in the Medshed. Now, in front of 102 peers and 100 staff, he IS Michael Jackson in his black and white jumpsuit, moon walking and executing splits and spins; and the boys and girls in the audience are on their feet, applauding what he is doing to express what they might or cannot.

  Two hours ago, this 3-foot high girl was getting her catheter dressing changed and lying down on a cute elephant-adorned examining table. Now she is centre-stage, surrounded by three supportive Caras, one holding a microphone, and she is a cheerleader with iridescent pom-poms, shouting her memorised lines between jumps, twists and rolls with a final toss of the pom-poms to the Caras. The audience is on its feet with applause.

  This boy an hour ago was a bald Irish kid with leukaemia, getting his central venous line flushed. Now, he is playing the tin-whistle flute as a solo, with his cottage friends on stage behind him, all dancing the Irish jig. He bows several times to the standing ovation. 'Cancer does not define who I am!' beams from his face.

Totals

Total visits today: 60 — 17 staff and 43 campers

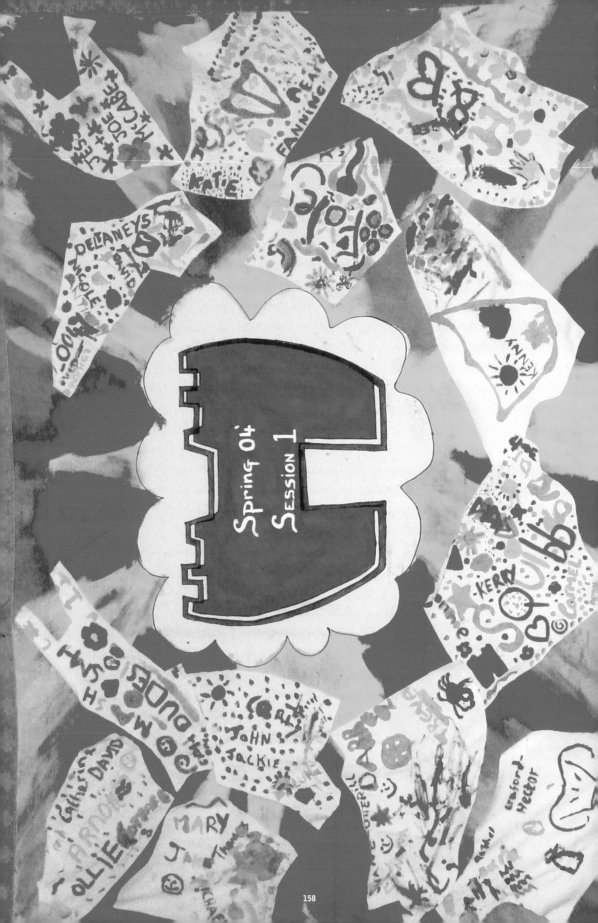

The Secret Garden

THE SECRET GARDEN

There is a secret garden in Barretstown. Nobody knows what the secret is. But I do. Mystical creatures live here on this beautiful grass, which is covered with dew every morning. I hope nobody will find out who these wonderful, magic creatures are, because that would be fatal, because they keep the balance. We would not be safe without them either. I know the secret ways, but if anybody else knew them, that would be disaster. I know these creatures and they fascinate me with their openness and sincerity. I have already seen them. I feel the power of life, that they have given to me — the secret they have shown me. The essence of life. With the clearest spring water.

Although I know that they can read our minds, it doesn't worry me. I have found harmony. I have found the language that is understood by everybody. The language of the ancient song.

I do not know what that power is, but I know it is good. I will follow the voice of it.

(Originally in Hungarian)

The Secret of Barretstown

This story takes place 1,200 years ago…

At that time, Barretstown was just a very huge castle and also the big garden was a mysterious secret. Unique creatures and fairies lived there. King Bass created the secret garden. It was said that people who went into this garden never came back. The lake was full of strange animals that looked like dragons. To tell the truth, most who went into the garden came back but they were drunk and talked rubbish. Near the castle there was a huge cave in which the dragon Barres lived. He did not really live — most of the time he slept, because a mysterious magician made him sleep with the help of a magical powder. There is much more to tell, but you will hear it in the course of the story.

Hagi was a farmer and there was a knight, Alex of Barretstown. Hagi wanted to be a knight as well, but before he could become a knight he had to serve the king.

Ten years passed by and he was 17 years old. Now he had to pass exams to become a knight. The test was to put magic powder on the nose of the dragon, when the first snow fell.

Hagi waited and waited until the first snow fell. He took his sleigh and a packet with the powder and he left.

When he arrived at the cave, he asked himself, 'Am I really going to go in?' His legs were shivering. But he went in. He took one step after another. Then he heard a roar. He dropped the packet. He ran and ran and ran. When he arrived at Barretstown, he was welcomed like a king. Everybody said that he was the biggest and bravest of all. So he gave in to temptation and hid behind his lie.

(Originally in German)

Somewhere in Barretstown
Gang Camp there is a secret
garden. It is called the
secret garden, but a lot of
people know about it.
    The secret garden is full
of fantasy and fairytales.
In the garden are many fine
flowers and greenhouses;

I

there is a high wall around
it and two beautiful gates.
Right now I'm sitting in the
garden hidden in some
bushes. I think the garden
is very nice. Why don't
you come and take a
look yourself!

(Originally in Norwegian)

l for

ver

RES

The Secret of the Secret's Secret

The lord of the secret garden
has a secret lunch and serves
secret bread at the secret lunch.
He prepared the lunch and
lives in a secret mill and this
secret mill has a secret power.
The secret of his secret power
nobody knows, except those
who eat the secret bread with
the lord of the secret garden.
There is secret wheat in the
secret garden, secret wheat goes
to the mill and this is very
dangerous.
The secret mill grinds the
secret wheat and gets power
and every secret night, the
secret mill starts working.

The secret bread will be made from the secret wheat and the lord of the secret garden can eat it. This way the lord also gets more magical power.

That is the way of the magically wonderful secret garden.

(Originally in Hungarian)

167

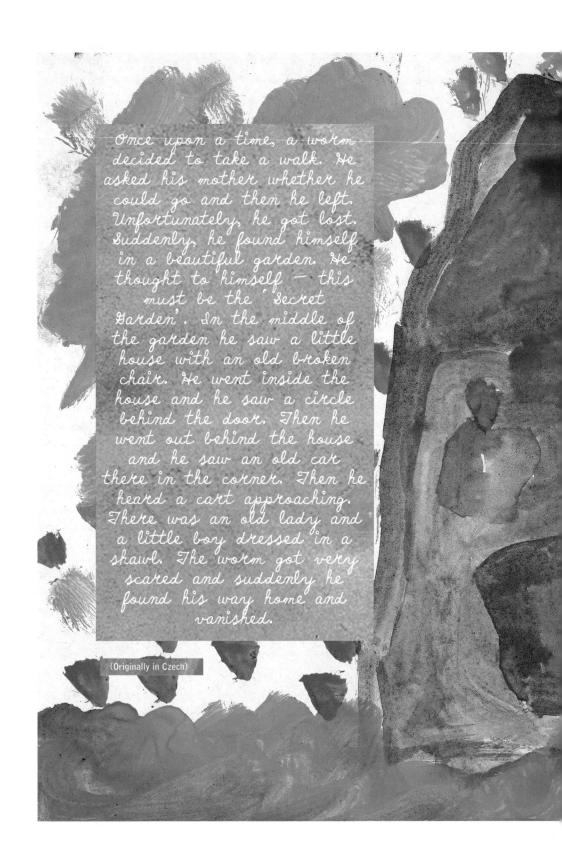

Once upon a time, a worm decided to take a walk. He asked his mother whether he could go and then he left. Unfortunately, he got lost. Suddenly, he found himself in a beautiful garden. He thought to himself — this must be the 'Secret Garden'. In the middle of the garden he saw a little house with an old broken chair. He went inside the house and he saw a circle behind the door. Then he went out behind the house and he saw an old cat there in the corner. Then he heard a cart approaching. There was an old lady and a little boy dressed in a shawl. The worm got very scared and suddenly he found his way home and vanished.

(Originally in Czech)

Day nine

9.20 a.m.
The Italian haemophilia brotherhood come in for their infusions.
Thanks to Luca, all six now self-infuse, whereas before camp, only
three had that skill.

10.20 a.m.
Our regular visitor is back again. This time, he caught his finger in
the door, unnoticed by anyone else. He says it hurts but there is also
a smile when he says it. After we establish there is no danger due to
his haemophilia, he smiles and says, 'Maybe I like the atmosphere of
this Medshed.'

11 a.m.
I leave Maria in charge as I have been invited to give a Grand Rounds
at 1 p.m. at the large teaching hospital in Dublin. My talk is titled:
'New Models for the Doctor–Patient Relationship: Significant Effects
of the Internet on Healthcare Delivery'.

6 p.m.
Tonight, dinner is arranged quite differently. Instead of the usual
individual tables, the tables are connected in a continuous large
rectangle. After eating, the recognition ceremony for the Caras and
translators who have been with the children for nine days begins. The
children wildly cheer the Caras, especially from their own cottage.
The kitchen staff, too, are recognised to wild applause.
  The Medshed – four nurses and two physicians – also receive a
certificate of appreciation and we manage to get some 'high fives',
especially from the frequent flyers who visited the Medshed more than
their fair share.

7.40 p.m.
We adjourn to the theatre where the children are seated and
recognition of special projects is made. This year, the dance and

theatre projects have been videotaped and are projected onto the large
screen. The children shout and cheer in appreciation of what their
fellow campers have accomplished. Awards and displays of the crafts
and artwork are also made.

Then a slide-show of 300 photos, taken from the 3,000 which were
shot during this week, are projected onto the screen. One shot after
another reminds and documents to the children what they looked like,
experienced and conquered: face paint, archery, silly hats, games,
horseback, canoeing, high ropes, low ropes, cottage shots of each
group. My fervent wish is that there could be a way to show the
parents of these children, and the parents who cannot yet let their
children leave home and go to camp, what the experience was like.

Barretstown has given a lot of thought and structure to how this
last-night closing ceremony should be. The camp director, Jules, and
the Caras explain that the thoughts and wishes and feelings and
personal experiences that the children wrote about today are put in a
magical pond in the centre of the theatre, surrounded by grass and
candles. In exchange for those thoughts on their experiences, they
each receive a small pebble that they can keep as a remembrance from
the castle. That pebble can take their memories back to the experience
any time they choose… And if the pebble is lost, the experience is
theirs to return to at will.

As this is translated, many of these young children become quiet and
some cry while sitting, or rush out, embarrassed. But the Caras
support them and, at the end of the service, we all gather in a
circle, hold hands and sing a simple, nostalgic Gaelic song that most
have learned. And that ends the last night of camp.

'Roger the Pirate' and Other Adventure Stories

THE TRIBAL CHALLENGE

One day the wizard came to us crying
because he had lost his magic blanket.
Later we found out that the tribal people
took it. They said that they would give it back
if we could complete their challenges and
impress the tribal chief. We had lots of fun
doing the challenges and we impressed the
tribal people and the chief. After the
challenges we got to see the chief and it was
a chicken! Though the chief was impressed
he would not give the magic blanket back.
The tribal people thought this was not fair so
they left him on his own. When the wizard
put the chief in a bin, he gave up and we got
the magic blanket back. The wizard was very
grateful and gave us all sweets.

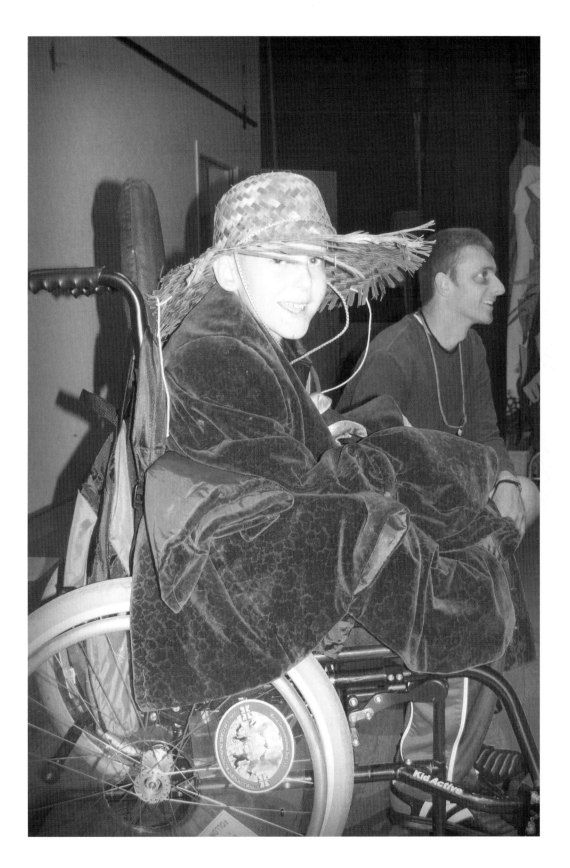

One day, Honmay from the

planet Riknae found out about the biggest criminal
organisation in history. Honmay was surprised to find
out about something as horrible as this in the
peaceful planet Riknae. He flew over in his hover-car
to where he knew the gang hid out. He climbed the
building and slipped in through the window and
someone entered the room. He hid under the table
and held onto the top of it. The person was unable to
see from under the table. But he could see his feet. He
was opening a drawer and Honmay saw him lift up a
sphere. He inserted the sphere in a stone tablet — the
sphere changed shape and started to change the shape
of the stone. Honmay felt a chill going down his spine
when whoever it was left the room. Honmay waited
for a few minutes before following. Honmay left the
room and entered a huge hallway. There seemed to be
millions of doors and he had no idea what door to
pick. He chose one to his left. He was in another
hallway and he heard a door close shut but when he
looked, there was nobody there. He ran to the door
and opened it, but when he looked inside, he
immediately noticed that he was trapped in a small
cube-shaped room, but there was a trap door in the
ceiling. He climbed though the trap door and heard a
clicking sound. Honmay turned around and saw three
goons. He was scared and he was afraid to move. The
goons tried to grab him but they all missed. One of
the goons fell down and the other two kept coming for
Honmay but they kept missing as Honmay was too
fast. Honmay climbed out and closed the trap door
behind him. Honmay was pleased with himself for
obviously defeating three goons in five seconds.

Honmay ran through the nearest door and when he looked again he saw three more goons and he easily defeated them too. Honmay ran for the further door and saw another group of three goons. He was so scared he almost fainted, but one saw Honmay and followed him through the last door. The goon ran at the same time as Honmay jumped and the goon ran under him. Honmay ran through the nearest door and he saw the guy who owned the sphere and what used to be the sphere and the stone tablet but was now a weapon. He and his partner in crime held the weapon together and shot a laser bullet at Honmay which missed. Honmay charged at the gang leaders and the fight was on! The fight went on for ages and Honmay destroyed the laser but the gang leaders were able to fight him without it. Honmay made duplicates of them and finally defeated one of them. The last guy and the remaining goons flew off in a giant hover-car and Honmay was disappointed that he hadn't got all of the goons, but he brought the goons he captured to the police and went home.

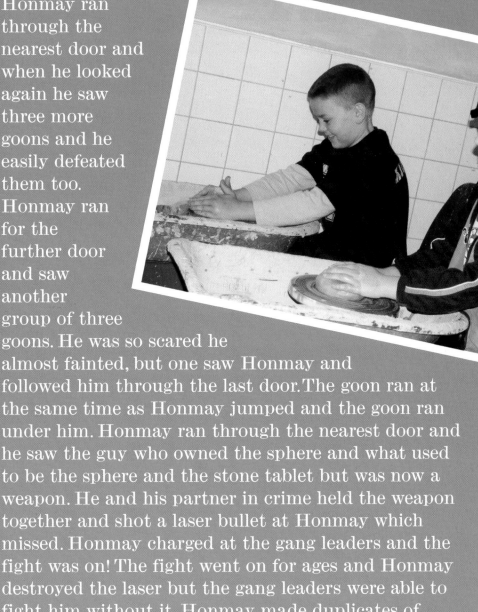

Roger the Pirate

Roger the pirate was very smart and well known. He won all the naval battles and robbed many ships and finally became the most dangerous pirate in the world. He was small, had a huge beard, one eye and a wooden leg. Roger the pirate had a parrot named Polly, who always accompanied him during his battles and raids.

(Originally in Polish)

The Legend of Cottage 2

There was once a huge, dark wood. Near it was a small village called Ballymore. The villagers were terrified to go into the woods. They had heard that a lot of men had gone into the woods and not returned. It was said that an evil spirit lived in the woods.

One day a courageous man came, who wanted to rid the woods of the spirit. He was called AJ. The leader of the village warned him not to go into the woods. However, AJ was so brave and had so many adventures with his donkey, Bas, he went without hesitation into the forest.

After some time, he heard something moving in the undergrowth. He took his sword in his hand and followed the rustling. It become louder and louder. Suddenly, a dwarf jumped out of the bushes. AJ was startled and wanted to grab the creature.

The dwarf cried out, 'If you let me live, I will give you three wishes.'

AJ put his sword back in its scabbard and said, 'If that is so, my first wish is that you come with me and be my assistant. Then you'll always have enough to eat and drink.' AJ asked the dwarf his name and the dwarf answered, 'I'm called Conor!'

The pair decided to keep looking for the spirit. They rode on together on Bas, naturally! That evening they were both very hungry. They rode on to the next telephone booth and rang the pizza parlour. They ordered a family-size pizza with extra cheese, anchovies, garlic, salami and pepperoni. They had to wait eight minutes until the pizza man arrived and surprised them.

It was Cicil, Conor's brother. They chatted for half an hour about anchovy pizza and make-up. By the time they started to eat, the pizza was stone cold. AJ used his second wish. The pizza became warm.

By midnight, the evil spirit began to disturb them. In front of AJ stood his mother, her hair in curlers. Suddenly AJ woke up and saw his mother, still standing there, saying, 'You had a bad dream.'

(Originally in German)

Nightmare

In the middle of the day I was on my boat and I was in my swimsuit and a magic wizard came and said, 'You have come into my sea.'

'I didn't know, sorry, it is too late now.'

With a wave of his wand he made a wave 25 feet high and with a crash my boat split into two. Then the wizard started flying and making a storm. It was so powerful it dragged me under the water. It pushed me 500 metres under water and on my way down I saw sharks, whales and fish going into a small hole. So I decided to go in, so I did. But a giant squid appeared in front of me and that is the last I remember. Then I was waking up in a whale's stomach and I woke up because of Pinocchio and his maker.

I Was Kidnapped by Pirates

Once, when I was swimming in the sea, I saw a big, black ship. It was a pirate ship. The leader of the pirates had a wooden leg and one eye. They brought me to my island and waited for me to tell them about the treasure. But I did not tell them.

Then they threatened me with many things like feeding me to the sharks or leaving me on a deserted island. I was most frightened when they threatened to throw me into a volcano. I was very scared. And almost told them...

But fortunately I realised a ship was coming. It was full of 'good' pirates. There was a battle and the 'good' pirates won.

In the end they brought me back to the island.

And that is all I have to say about that.

(Originally in Hungarian)

The Two Rings Dog

IN THE BARRETSTOWN CAMP, situated in Ireland, there was a castle in which people used to say there was a ghost that makes kids disappear. Another story that people used to have about the castle was that there was a witch that turned the kids into pigs and afterwards ate them. But none of them were bad tales if you compare them with this one.

Beside the castle there is a dog with two rings and when it gets dark at night, and there is a full moon, he turns into a wolfman. Any kid who tried to put a ball though the rings, laugh at him or do any other thing that would annoy him would be punished by being his slave for eternity.

Everybody in the village knew about the story because it passed from one generation to another. People used to tell it in the school, in church, on the local TV and in the local newspaper. But there was a gang of kids that used to laugh at everybody in the village. They used to set fire to houses, schools and all kinds of buildings. They used to break into houses and rob and they didn't believe in the dog story at all. One night they decided to go to the castle and take the dog from the stone where he was and drag him to the lake and throw him in the water. When they arrived there, they set about pulling him out of the stone. The bad thing was that the statue was heavier than they thought. Night was close so they had to leave it for the next night. The darkness covered the Barretstown sky. The moon let herself be seen, but is was not a FULL MOON. The statue came to life but it didn't do anything to the kids because it had a good plan. The next day when the hooligans went back to continue with their plan, the wolfman was waiting for them to give them their deserved punishment. A big fight began that lasted hours but the wolf won and the kids were condemned to be his slave for all eternity. And if you don't believe that it really happened, you should go to the castle, and find some bloody proof of that hard fight. But don't do anything to the dog — you could be the next victim.

(Originally in Spanish)

Pirates

A long time ago, on a small island called Kauii there peacefully lived a tribe of people. They were very rich, when one day something terrible happened. An armed ship full of greedy pirates attacked the island. They killed almost everyone, although a few injured managed to survive. One of the survivors (named Willy) whose family were all dead decided to attack the pirates with a team of others. He decided to build a ship to travel to the pirates. He found a rope and some weeds in the forest and constructed a boat. While he was sailing on the boat in the ocean, he saw a small cave. He decided to explore it. It was dark and cold inside and suddenly he heard a human voice. It was an old man looking for shelter. Willy decided to take him with him. Suddenly, they saw a huge wave and a whale appeared from it. The whale swallowed them together with the boat. They were terrified when they saw human bones inside. They thought it was the end. But the old man took a knife out of his pocket and stabbed the whale in the stomach. The whale jumped, made a very loud and deep voice, opened his jaws and spat the crew out. They flew high up into the air but they died anyway because they landed straight into the jaws of a shark.

(Originally in Polish)

The Story of a Magic Garden

There was a boy called Clac walking around his garden. Suddenly a ghost appeared and told him he would have to complete three very difficult challenges in order to get some powers. The boy was very happy and agreed, and so they went to the forest.

The first challenge was to walk over a bush with thorns. He had some trouble, but he managed in the end. The second challenge was to save a baby from a wolf's claws. He got some scratches but he could do it. The third challenge was much more difficult. It was to fight a bear. He did that too, but he almost died.

When he finished, the ghost gave him the powers and said to him, 'Since you have been so brave, I'll grant you three wishes.'

The first wish was to be handsome, the second was to have a girlfriend, and the third was to own a dog. In the end, the ghost went away and the boy kept the powers and had his wishes.

(Originally in Spanish)

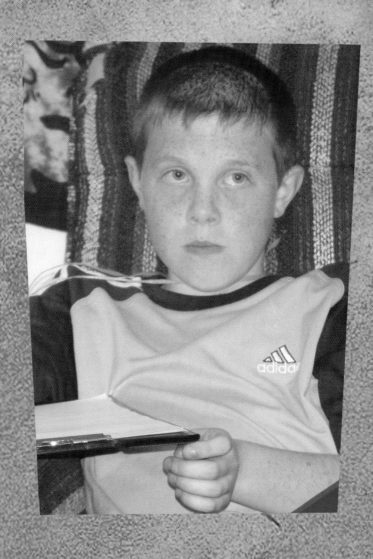

I looked behind me and it was still there so I swam as fast as I could. But then it caught up with me. It was a massive monster with three eyes, six hands and four legs. He ate me up in one go. I was wriggling around in his stomach when I met a huge

ship in his gut and other
people as well. I asked them
what they were doing here
but there was no reply. I tried
to get out but I could not.
We were trapped forever and
I knew that I was going to
die. Then I saw a bit of light
at the end of the tunnel and
I got through his bum. It
smelled rotten but I was
saved.

The Terrifying Adventure

Once upon a time, there was a group of kids who decided to go to a castle called 'Barretstown'. In this castle there was an evil witch called 'Matilda'. She used to turn children into pigs and then fry and

OWN

eat them. One day the kids formed a flag, the Barretstown flag, the only one that could defeat the witch. Those kids showed the flag to the witch and turned her into a kind and lovely girl again.

(Originally in Spanish)

OEATHORTH Island

Once upon a time, there was a peaceful and colourful island. It was completely different from all others because it was the shape of a parallelogram and smelled like exotic fruits. Many bad parrots lived there.

In order for someone to become chief, they had to be over the age of 20 years. And of course, they should be stronger than the other parrots, something that was very rare to their race. Every year there was a contest in which every parrot (over 20 years old) who wanted to be chief took part.

One year they had to do the contest twice because the previous chief wasn't doing his duties and the parrots' land wasn't doing well.

In the second contest, the winner was a parrot who was brave, strong, colourful and beautiful. His only disadvantage was that he talked too much and he was a dictator. That didn't bother the other parrots at all because, above all, he did his job well and that's why the next year they lived happily ever after on the island.

(Originally in Greek)

The island known as Ireland is located in the Atlantic Ocean. There are many underwater flowers, dolphins and sharks in the surrounding waters. The ocean is full of pirate ships — some are good and some are bad. There is a lot of sand in the ocean and the waves are very high.

Once the pirates lost their way and they landed on an

196

island. The pirates had no food, nothing to eat or drink; that is why they decided to eat fish and fruit. They managed to build houses there very slowly. Eventually the whole place became inhabited and the country of Ireland was formed. At present the island is heavily populated and lots of tourists visit every year.

The pirates still live there; they continue to catch fish, sharks and whales. They keep these animals in the zoo so that the people can also see them. People make different pills from the fat of the whales; as for the fish, they're simply eaten.

Pirates of the Caribbean —
The Curse of Great Creatures

The pirates left the port and sailed for a long time, until they ended up in the middle of the ocean. All of a sudden, the water in front of them opened up. A sea creature appeared, creeping out of the water. The lifeguard couldn't see the creature. After a while, a special instrument beeped. This instrument searches for other ships. The instrument continued to beep for a long time. Then the lifeguard noticed it. He called another lifeguard and they headed to look for the creatures. Finally they confronted him and that is the end of the story.

(Originally in Czech)

Day 10

4 a.m.

The first group of children from Cyprus and Jordan is down in the castle courtyard, sleepy and looking sad as they board their bus for Dublin Airport. Eimear and the nurses have worked hard to ensure that the translators and chaperones have the medications the children will need for their trip home.

For some, the 6- to 10-hour plane ride with changes will just be the beginning of the journey to reach home.

Most of the Caras are up, looking a bit tired themselves as some never went to sleep. They are out on the castle courtyard, encouraging 'their' children, taking last photographs, saying the last goodbyes, checking for things left behind, and waving to them, running alongside the bus as it leaves the courtyard and out the gate.

5.30 a.m.

The second group is ready to leave for the airport and the process will repeat itself twice more until noon. I am on that 5.30 a.m. bus. As we leave the Barretstown Castle grounds, two Caras are running and waving their hands at us. Almost as a scene from *Peter Pan*: my seat companion jumps up and down and says to his fellow camper, 'Wendy' across the narrow aisle: 'Look, they are waving at us and trying to catch us. They don't want to see us leave.' My heart sinks … but I am pulled to a different expression of the same feeling when the more militant 13-year-old behind me says: 'Maybe we can have a mutiny in the bus and stay another week.' I think camp was a success.

12 noon

The 35 Irish children will board the bus, the tearful goodbyes will take place, and Connor will drive them to three of the local hospitals in Dublin. There, anxious parents will await more experienced, older children, possibly changed from who they were ten days before.

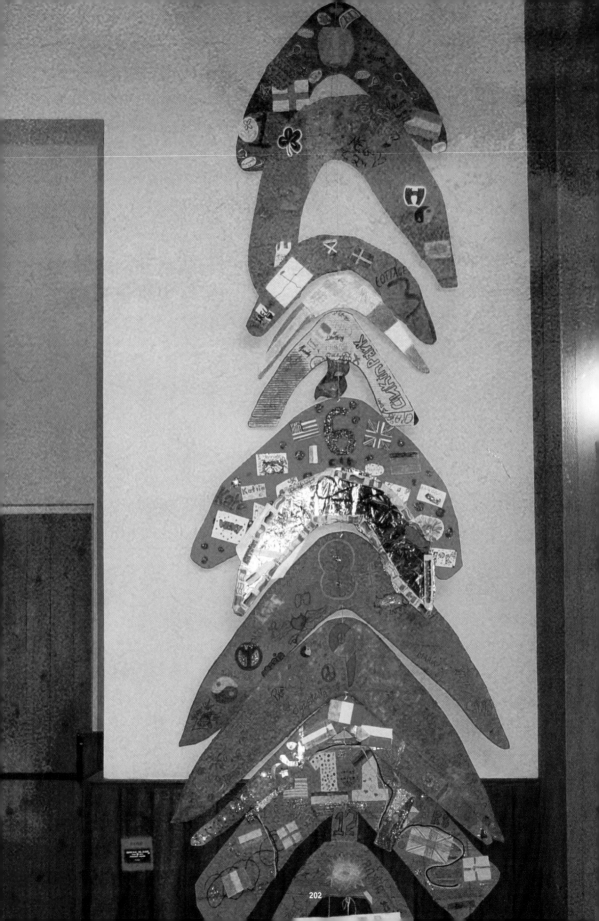

In a
World of
My Own

If somebody has gone,
Don't call him back.
The memory which started to fade
Is not bright any more.
If somebody has gone,
Don't cry.
It's easier to forget,
In somebody else's arms.
Believe me!
If the summer leaves your heart,
And the winter moves in,
Snow covers the hills,
Think about the past,
Which may be painful.
Sometimes you are betrayed,
But you need to love!
The one who says he adores you,
Don't believe him.
The one who says he loves you,
May be insincere.
But give your heart to the one who is silent,
Because the heart that is true doesn't talk — just loves!

(Originally in Hungarian)

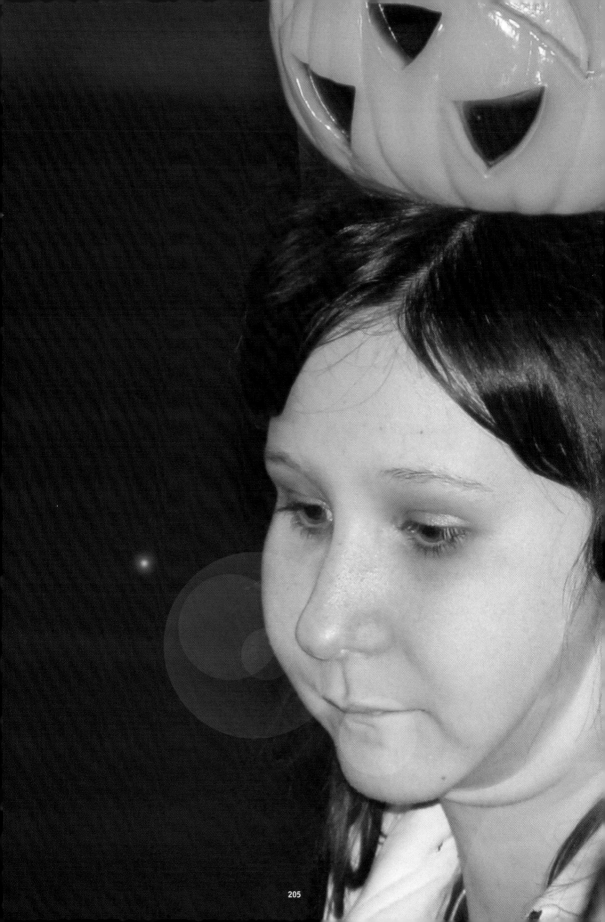

In a World of My Own

Sun always shining

Grass always green

Happy joyful faces

Always to be seen

Cure for illnesses

Cancer, asthma, many more

Stop enemies fighting

Help those that are poor

Stop the bullies

Who have nothing better to do

Calling you names

Always picking on you

Make our world bright

Full of faces filled with joy

Life is a gift

Don't treat it as a toy.

News travels fast
There's an old wreck in the overpass
Wine in a glass
And a well-travelled bed
Down the length and breadth of a
Motorway
Down the information highway
I took a ride in an angel's heap.

And you're leaving me
Behind in this life.

I found relief
It's taken me over
Where will I be
Adrift on the seas
And wheels fly over
Like an angel's heap.

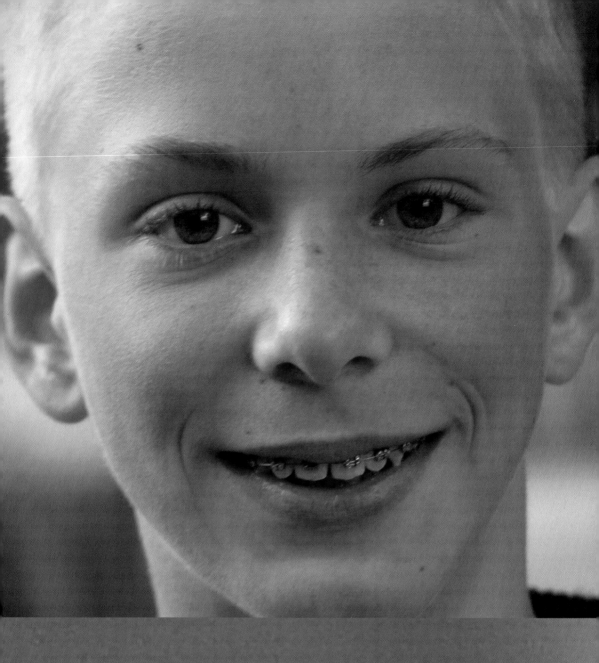

The sky is gorgeous, so bright and blue,
The sea is full of creatures I'd love to swim through.
The sky carries aeroplanes,
The sea carries remains.
Lost in the underworld of life it's so true.

I Wanted to Get Away

I wanted to get away from all the mayhem,
I wanted to get away, fly away to another
    world or dimension,
So I would be free of all the tension which
    lay before me, like a never-ending story.
So here I am today,
Hip Hip Hooray!
Now something new has been laid before me,
It's kind of like a never-ending story,
But of adventures and happiness for every
    different day.

I adore crafts and I prepared a figure out of gypsum. It stands on my shelf and I always talk to it when I am sad and it seems to understand and sometimes it seems to wink and blink. One summer's day I went to camp and I brought my figure with me too. Later, I was homesick, missing my Mom and Dad and sister and dog and everything. I lost my earrings, which were a present from my father and so were sentimental to me. I cried a lot. I wanted to go home and as always I turned to my figure. I told it what the problem had been and then something very strange happened. My figure sat up in a miraculous way (it had been lying down), so it sat up and stared at me astonished with a smiling face and said, 'Where is your happiness?'

'What?' I asked, thinking not of myself any more. 'Are you alive?'

'Of course,' it answered.

For a couple of minutes I was standing in front of it. In fact, I was sitting, as I could not stand because of my astonishment. Then it looked at me again, losing its smile, and asked me, rather annoyed, 'Can't you hear? I am talking to you.'

Then I stopped being surprised, as I didn't want to make it angry. I wasn't crying any more, just sniffling sometimes, and I gave a sigh and answered, 'I miss my family!'

'Don't be sad; you will never be as happy as here, just make use of it.' We were chatting! I was deep in thought — how could it speak to me, how could it come to life? It said that it had been the creature of fantasy of every child and sometimes of adults, which helped them to be happy and merry. 'We were made by humans, more and more of us are living and the only important thing is to believe in us.' I couldn't speak any more as the door opened suddenly and I started to look at my legs without thinking. The figure was in the same lying position as before and my friend came in, and she hugged me and asked me to come and play. 'OK,' I answered, and forgot about the strange event. In the evening it occurred to me again and I wondered had I dreamt it or not. Had it been true or not? I thought for a while and then I fell asleep and I dreamt of my figurine.

(Originally in Hungarian)

There was an elf called Green Leaf. He had very yellow teeth.

He was always clumsy, until he met his mumsy.

He was very happy therefore, and not clumsy any more.

His mom took him fishing at the moor, Green Leaf had never been before.

He caught the biggest fish, and ate it in a dish.

Afterwards, he was full, so he fell asleep on a bull.

Later he was thankful to his mumsy, for stopping him from being clumsy.

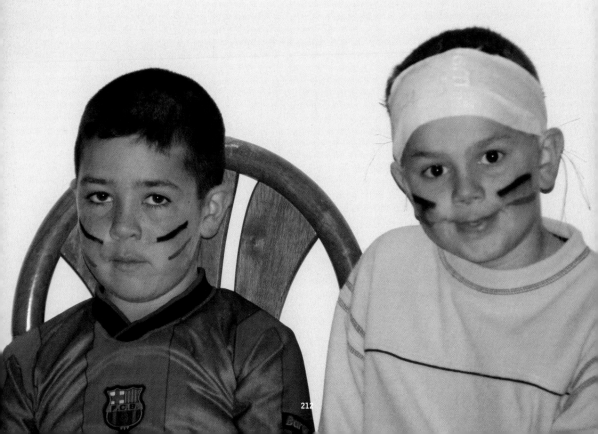

B laid stick in the mud
A nd caught a fish
R ode a horse
R went to bed when he was told
E slept out in a tent
T old a joke
S lept for an hour
T lost his teddy
O got upset
W on the pillow fight
N eeded his tablet

My Net

Today I found this rugged and worn out net in the Secret Garden.

The net is green in colour and has holes all over it.

It is an old and unused net which is in misery.

Before I took this net it obviously had a past life which came to a sad ending but what that was will always be a mystery. A net just hanging off a pillar thinking of the good times which now have turned sour. It probably once was a fine new net but now it is just full of holes and worn-out grass so it could have been a net for a goal post but we don't know.

This old net should be reused to put it out of its misery so it can relive the good times.

This is my story of an old net with no life.

Being happy in the morning, laughing,
Waking up with a smile on your face.
Getting so much energy from life,
Feeling forever young.

(Originally in German)

More than 10,000 children with serious illnesses and their families have benefited from Barretstown's life-changing programmes since it opened in 1994.

Everything is provided free, including round-trip airfares.

More than 12,000 new cases of childhood cancer are diagnosed in Europe each year. Barretstown would love to help many more children.

Our unique Serious Fun programmes currently cost €4.4 million to run each year.

We have the facilities, we have the backing of the medical world — now all we need are the funds to bring more children to Barretstown.

If you would like to become involved in Barretstown's work, through fundraising, making a regular donation or volunteering, please call 00 353 45 864 115.

Thank you!

Barretstown
Barretstown Castle
Ballymore Eustace
Co. Kildare
Ireland
Telephone 00353 45 864 115
Fax 00353 45 864 197
www.barretstown.org